Love is Blonde

Hortense Ullrich

Love is Blonde

Aus dem Deutschen
von Helena Ragg-Kirkby

Thienemann

Tuesday 17th October

Wow. Oh wow. He is magnificent. Honestly.

He's perfect. Ideal. He's a **knockout**.

I'm totally crazy about him.

It's completely *knocked me over.* Literally. In the true sense of the word. I'm quite serious.

I went crashing onto the floor right in front of him. Lying at his feet, so to speak. Ha ha ha. Honestly. It was so-o-o-o embarrassing.

Today I was **marching** through town, because my mother had sent me off to buy some **loo paper**.

"Make it the big packet, please. The one with thirty-two rolls, Jojo!"

I hate that. Quite apart from looking like a Mexican pack-donkey, buying loo roll is *so* embarrassing. The big packets don't fit into a shopping bag, and I'm guaranteed to be the only teenager in the whole town who has to cart around twenty kilos of

---

he's a knockout – er ist umwerfend;
to march – im Stechschritt laufen; loo paper – Klopapier

loo paper in full view of the general public. At any rate, I was totally fed up, and just wanted to get home as quickly as possible.

Then I saw him. He looked so cool! Totally gorgeous!! Wow, I was totally **smitten**. My heart lost its rhythm; it stumbled.

And, a minute later, so did I. Over a **dog-lead**. I hadn't seen it, because I had been staring so **raptly** at the guy the whole time.

I was probably smiling as I fell, and I must have still been smiling when I was lying on the ground, because he said: "You smile like an angel."

I glowed even more. My knee felt damp. But I didn't look at it: I was too fascinated by Mr Wonderful.

He smiled charmingly, adding: "A fallen angel." Then he bent down and helped me back onto my feet. My knee started to hurt. But I couldn't stop looking at his eyes. What's more, I tried to stop *him* looking at *me*, so that he didn't see the loo rolls. That would have been *so* embarrassing.

He looked at my hair and said: "Well, all right … if you were blonde."

Huh? What was he talking about?

"I *am* blonde!" I **defended** myself.

He laughed politely. "Mousey brown."

---

to be smitten – verknallt sein; dog-lead – Hundeleine; rapt – hingerissen; to defend (oneself) – (sich) verteidigen

"Mousey blonde!" I cried **indignantly**.

What was I on about? Why *mousey* blonde?

"Blonde!" I corrected myself.

The charmer smiled even more charmingly. My knee stung like hell. Something wet was slowly running down my leg. With my good leg, I tried **surreptitiously** to kick the loo rolls behind me.

"Angels are platinum blonde," he instructed me.

Aha. *He* should know.

What actually *is* platinum blonde? And who's interested?

Me! Because the guy looked so unbelievably mega-gorgeous. And because he was so totally cool!

He gave me an even nicer smile and looked at my knee. "Oh, you're injured. It's bleeding."

"No-o-o-o," I said in a somewhat strained voice, as I was by now having to **grit my teeth**, because my knee was starting to hurt terribly. But I thought: it's totally uncool to be injured.

I looked at my knee. It was bleeding. And how!

"It's just paint," I heard myself saying, and asked myself who on earth would believe such nonsense. At best, someone with the IQ of a **garlic clove**.

"Oh, right," said Prince Charming, and smiled in a friendly manner.

---

indignant – empört, aufgebracht; surreptitious – verstohlen; to grit one's teeth – die Zähne zusammenbeißen; garlic clove – Knoblauchzehe

Wow, what a smile! Hopefully he hadn't seen the loo paper.

"I have to go," he said apologetically, gesticulating towards a dog that was standing next to him.

"Aaaargh!" I cried, shocked, and jumped back, full of disgust. Or, rather, I **hobbled** back on account of my knee, and almost fell over the loo rolls.

I looked at the dog, horrified. It was a black poodle. But *what* a specimen: a giant poodle. "Has he been taking hormone tablets or what?" it slipped out of me.

The poodle looked like a body-builder. A blow-dried and curled bodybuilder. As ugly as sin. Super-bourgeois. Ten on the embarrassment scale.

The dog-owner frowned. "This is a King Poodle."

I grimaced. A King. Not a **bog-standard** poodle, of course. As ugly as sin. But a King! Your Majesty. How clumsy of me!

But then I gave myself a good telling off for having made my **loathing** of the giant creature so obvious. The way to a boy's heart is through his dog, that's for sure.

"Swee-e-e-e-t!" I said. Evidently rather unconvincingly, because he gave me a **baffled** look. I pointed vaguely at the mega-poodle. "The dog. I think he's sweet."

---

to hobble – humpeln; bog-standard – stinknormal;
loathing – Abscheu; baffled – verwirrt

The guy looked at me, horrified. "Seriously? Nobody's ever said that."

Oh God, what now?

"Well, all right, not *so* sweet. Just, well, you know … what's he called?" Good **diversionary tactic**.

"Herr Schmitt."

"Herr Schmitt?" And how, pray, are you supposed to respond to that? I didn't want to make yet another mistake. "Herr Schmitt," I repeated slightly foolishly, nodding in affirmation. Then I thought: if he's a *king* poodle, perhaps that should be Herr *von* Schmitt.

"Stupid name, don't you think?" asked the guy.

"Oh …" I said **evasively**.

"I'm just doing my Grandma a favour," he explained.

Now I was totally baffled.

"I take Herr Schmitt for a pee. Every afternoon. It's her dog. The old lady can't walk that well any more, and, well, I just help her out."

"Wow, that's so nice of you!" I was seriously impressed – the guy was totally lovely.

He laughed modestly. "**Get lost**! It's perfectly normal, isn't it?"

I nodded. "Sure."

"I have to go. Perhaps we'll meet again …" he said.

---

diversionary tactic – Ablenkungstaktik;
evasive – ausweichend; Get lost! – Sag bloß!

My heart leapt. I quickly put my hand over it so that nobody could see it jumping.

"I'm here every day," I stammered, inwardly shaking my head. What kind of nonsense was I talking?

"Okay, see you tomorrow, then." Prince Charming saluted me with a coolly raised hand.

Then he spotted the huge pack of loo paper. "Oh, don't forget your loo rolls," he said.

Argh! What now?

I looked at the mega-pack and heard myself saying: "That doesn't belong to me."

There I stood, denying Mum's loo paper. I felt like Judas.

"Oh, right. See you!" He saluted me again.

He was presumably waiting for me to go. But I couldn't go. I had to wait until he was out of sight so I could pick up the loo paper again and **cart** it home.

Or should I just leave it lying there and go home?

No. It would be just my luck for someone to pick it up and give it back to me, and that would be even more embarrassing.

So I stood there waiting.

He stood there waiting, too.

"I have to stay here. I've got to wait a bit. Don't feel you have to hang about," I suggested.

He laughed. "Okay, till tomorrow then." And then he went.

---

to cart – karren

I was just about to bend down to pick up the loo rolls when he turned round again. I shot back up and made out that nothing was **amiss**.

"Platinum blonde would really suit you," he called to me by way of goodbye.

I stood **as if rooted to the spot**. Had he seen me about to pick up the loo rolls?

No-o-o, definitely not. Hopefully not.

I can't believe it! The coolest boy in town has agreed to meet me. Tomorrow. Oh, wow, am I a lucky cow or what? It's just too brilliant to be true! And he's at least three years older than me. And guys like that aren't normally the tiniest bit interested in girls of my age.

I stood there for a bit longer, looking longingly after him.

Then I took myself off to the **chemist's**.

The assistant saw my knee, gave me a really sympathetic look, and said: "You'd like a **dressing**?"

"No-o-o," I said. "**Hair dye**. Platinum blonde, please."

---

to be amiss – nicht in Ordnung sein;
as if rooted to the spot – wie angewurzelt;
chemist – Drogerie; dressing – (hier:) Verband;
hair dye – Haarfärbemittel

Wednesday 18th October

"Oh my God, Jojo darling, what have you done to yourself?" cried my mother this morning, shocked by my appearance.

Darling? I don't believe it. The woman just won't learn. I hate it when she calls me darling.

"Oh, it's already **on the mend**," I said, looking at my knee.

"I don't think so," said my mother, looking at my hair.

Oh three cheers. That's motherly love for you. I come hobbling along with a great big bandage round my knee, and all she can look at is my hair. Platinum blonde. I dyed it yesterday evening.

"Was that a mistake, or did you do it on purpose?" asked my mother.

"Did you lose a bet, or what?" **smirked** my eight-year-old sister Flippi.

Flippi's main task in her chaotic young life is to drive me mad with irritation. There should be a law that quite simply forbids the existence of little sisters.

I'd tried everything. Ages ago, when Flippi was still a small child, I had tried exchanging her for a dog, selling her at the **flea market**, and – three times – "forgetting" to bring her home from the

---

to be on the mend – heilen; to smirk – schmunzeln;
flea market – Flohmarkt

playground. **To no avail**. Somehow she'd always managed to find her way back to us. It was hopeless. Quite soon it became clear to me that I would just have to live with this sister for a couple of years.

My mother often felt pretty desperate about it too, though mostly she just said cautiously: "Just wait, Jojo, you'll be the best of friends one day – you'll see. It's just a matter of time and good will."

"**Put** Flippi **up for adoption**, and I promise I'll be her best friend!" I offered my mother.

But this suggestion also threw her into the depths of despair. She was totally devastated, and ploughed through countless parenting guidance books. Firstly she blamed herself, then my father, as he'd **scarpered** when Flippi arrived. Ever since then, my mother has been convinced that Flippi and I are bound to display all sorts of signs of extreme psychological damage. Because we are, so to speak, growing up without a father. She's always very disappointed when she **trogs off** with us to some expert or another who then tells her that Flippi and I are totally normal. A bit more chaotic than average, they say, but that has nothing to do with her being a single mother.

My mother, though, sticks to her theory. Then

---

to no avail – es half alles nicht;
to put a child up for adoption – ein Kind zur Adoption freigeben; to scarper – abhauen; to trog off – hintrotten

the experts take a deep breath and say: "Frau Sonntag, how would you feel about us having a little chat? Just you and me, without the children."

My mother is totally outraged every time. "What's that supposed to mean? Do you think there's something the matter with me? Honestly! I'm here because of the children. I'm a worried mother. I don't believe it!" Then she stands up demonstratively. "Right, children, we're off!" And she sweeps out of the **surgery**.

There you go. In any case, Flippi was annoying me as always, and in this situation I certainly didn't need stupid comments from an eight-year-old.

"Wow, what planet do you live on? Platinum blonde is totally in," I told the pair of them.

"Is it going to go out again?" my mother wanted to know.

"What do you mean, 'go out'? Jojo's hair colour is already out!" Flippi stated expertly. Then she turned to my mother. "If I do something so stupid when I'm thirteen, please shoot me."

My mother brushed her aside. "Just leave it, Filipine. Jojo doubtless has her reasons for it."

"Have I ever," I nodded triumphantly, looking **gratefully** at my mother.

Flippi rolled her eyes. Then she suddenly gave

---

surgery – (Arzt-)Praxis; grateful – dankbar

herself a slap on the head. “I get it! I know why Jojo looks as if she’s about to sign up with the coastguard service as a **light-buoy**. She’s got to impress some brain-dead **whippersnapper**. Hopefully Jojo’s puberty will soon be over.”

Flippi always talked about it as if it were an illness.

I **blushed**.

My mother smirked at me. “Love is blonde, isn’t it?”

Oh **blimey**, now she’s at it as well!

I was totally indignant. “Hey, just listen …”

“Nah. Love is just blind!” stated Flippi.

I shall set off with this sentence ringing in my ears. Set off to meet the love of my life. This time it has to be great love. I’m absolutely sure of it.

Love is blind! Flippi doesn’t have a clue. Just wait until she’s my age!

I hope he won’t have the dog with him today – normally, anyone would hesitate to be seen in public with a dog like that.

Or, at least, anyone who’s got more taste than a **gnat**.

---

light-buoy – Leuchtboje;
whippersnapper – Bürschchen; to blush – erröten;
blimey! – du meine Güte!; gnat – Mücke

Thursday 19th October

The dog is kind of okay after all. If you get to know him better and all that. I didn't find him quite so horrible yesterday either. It's quite possible that it's the next mega-cool thing and totally trendy to go around with a **weird** creature like that. You never know.

Oh, it was so-o-o-o-o-o-o-o-o brilliant yesterday.

Eberhard and I – (yes, he is actually called Eberhard. Sorry, nobody's perfect. But once you've got used to it, the name definitely doesn't sound so weird. And that coming from a "Josefine" – hahaha) anyway, Eberhard and I spent the whole of yesterday afternoon taking Herr Schmitt out together. Amazing or what?!

Oh, it was so brilliant. He is so-o-o-o-o sweet! Eberhard, that is, not the dog. God, I can hardly write the name, the name is truly … um, let's say it takes some getting used to.

If you saw him, you'd never guess that he was called Eberhard. Honestly you wouldn't. He's totally lovely and funny and interesting.

So, anyway, I went to town yesterday to meet Eberhard.

He almost didn't spot me. Platinum blonde as I now am.

---

weird – unheimlich, merkwürdig

He walked past me, and I called: "Hey!"

He stopped, looked at me wide eyed, and said: "Oh, it's you. I don't believe it! You've dyed your hair!"

I nodded, turned somewhat red, and said proudly: "Platinum blonde!"

He grinned and repeated: "Platinum blonde." He grinned even more broadly, then stopped grinning and said most charmingly: "It looks really cool. Suits you. It gives you an …" He searched for the words.

"… An **angelic air**?" I came to his aid.

He nodded and grinned again. Then he turned serious. "My blonde angel," he said, and my insides melted.

This is great love. A clear case.

"Do you want to walk with us for a bit? Herr Schmitt hates standing around."

"Fine," I said, looking fondly at Herr Schmitt. He did at least bring us together. This giant creature is, so to speak, our Cupid.

I attempted to stroke him. The dog, that is, not the guy. With a dog that size, you don't even have to bend down – you just have to raise your arm slightly. A child of Flippi's height would be somewhere around the dog's eye level. And that would really scare the dog. Guaranteed.

---

angelic air – engelhafte Ausstrahlung

Anyway, I wanted to stroke him – the dog – but the **mutt** growled at me. I quickly withdrew my hand and smiled uncertainly at my dream prince.

"He likes you."

I was absolutely astonished. "Are you sure?"

"Of course," nodded Mr Wonderful. "Do you want to hold his lead?" he offered, holding it out to me.

I bravely grasped the lead, which Herr Schmitt **graciously** tolerated.

"Suits you," stated Eberhard.

"This hair colour?" I asked.

He shook his head. "The dog. That looks kind of cool. You and a King Poodle."

I glowed, and felt pretty proud.

"If you want, you can hold him the whole time," he offered generously.

I was totally thrilled. "Seriously?"

"Of course," he nodded graciously.

Wow, I was completely blown away. There I was, walking along with the coolest guy in town, and he was letting me hold his King Poodle's lead. How lucky can you get?

"What school do you go to?" I asked.

"Humboldt."

"What a shame." It just slipped out.

"Why?"

"Erm…" I could hardly say 'because I don't go to

---

mutt – Köter; gracious – gnädig

the same school.' So what now? "Erm… because … they're supposed to be pretty strict there."

"You're right." He nodded. "It really gets on your nerves."

"What's your name?" I quizzed him further. You need to get the important facts straight right **at the outset**.

He hesitated, then grinned. "Eberhard," he said, drawing the word out. Then he waited.

I swallowed. Just don't make any comments. 'Eberhard' really **was the pits**. But he couldn't help it.

"And how old are you?" I quickly asked. Nothing much could go wrong with that.

"Sixteen," he replied.

Wow, sixteen is really old. "So'm I …, soon," I said, thinking: it's not a lie. I am going to be sixteen. In three years' time.

"You look younger," he stated.

"I know," I **sighed**. Probably about thirteen.

"What are your hobbies?" I tried to change the subject.

He **shrugged his shoulders**. "I don't have much time for hobbies. I'm always busy with something. How about you?"

---

at the outset – am Anfang; to be the pits – ätzend sein, die Härte sein; to sigh – seufzen;
to shrug one's shoulders – mit den Achseln zucken

I shrugged my shoulders too. If I knew what he thought was good, I'd immediately take it up as a hobby. But as it was, I had to remain a bit vague.

"Music?" I tried cautiously.

He nodded. "Hmm."

That evidently didn't hit the spot. Second attempt: "Sport."

He appeared surprised. "Seriously?"

The fact that he seemed so surprised irritated me. Do I look *that* unsporty?

"Absolutely!" I said defiantly.

"What sport, then?" he wanted to know.

Now I needed something cool, something exotic. I had to think for a moment.

"Don't you know what kind of sport you're into?" he said, surprised.

"Yes, of course I do," I retorted. Whilst still thinking like mad. "I just don't like talking about it that much," I said, in order **to stall for time**.

"Okay." He dropped the subject.

Now, that was stupid, because something had just occurred to me. "Well, I can tell *you.* I do **fencing**," I said proudly.

"Seriously? Like musketeers?"

"Exactly!" I **beamed**. "But without the costume," I added, just to be on the safe side.

---

to stall for time – Zeit gewinnen; fencing – Fechten;
to beam – strahlen

"Cool," he said.

Oh! A winner.

"**Sword** or **foil**?"

Argh, he knows what he's talking about. And I don't. So all I said was: "Depends." Then I went on: "Herr Schmitt is really sweet."

He looked at the dog and shrugged his shoulders. "He's all right."

By then I had run out of things to say. I thought: it's his turn now. He could say something too.

"I think it's really nice of you to walk through the park with me. It's pretty **dreary**. **Trudging** around day after day with that mutt, um, that dog," the coolest guy in town suddenly said, and I went red right to the roots of my dyed hair.

He thinks it's really nice of me! That means he thinks *I'm* nice, doesn't it? I wasn't prepared for that. What are you supposed to say?

"I like doing it. I mean, I always go for walks anyway. It's one of my hobbies. And doing it like this, with a dog, is actually a lot nicer," I said, turning even redder. Because of course I didn't mean it was nicer with the dog, but nicer with him. But I really didn't want to say that now.

And then I felt terribly excited again. That really was a hit: me, walking through the park with the

---

sword – Degen, Schwert; foil – Florett;
dreary – öde, langweilig; to trudge – (mühselig) stapfen

coolest guy in town. Wow, I was so excited. I was hoping the whole time that we'd **bump into** someone from my class. I wished someone could see me now.

Otherwise, I'll just tell Lucilla. I'll swear her to secrecy, naturally. That way I can be sure that she'll pass it on to everyone else.

Lucilla is actually really nice. She just has a way about her that sometimes **gets on my nerves**.

"Oh, Josie," she always pipes. "Your life is so exciting. There's always something happening to you."

She is, of course, right, but she has no idea how much that irritates me. For every excitement in my life always ends in catastrophe and with me wanting to sink into the ground with embarrassment.

I've never worked out why that should be the case, but I have gradually got used to it, and I already know not to expect anything different.

But this time, it's going to be **ace**. I can feel it for sure. Eberhard is a dream guy (the name apart). And he's going out for walks with me. Absolutely nothing can go wrong.

"Do you know anything about dogs?" His question interrupted my chain of thought.

"Of course," I said at once. What is there to know? They bark, eat, and go for pees. End of story.

---

to bump into sb – zufällig jmdn. treffen;
otherwise – ansonsten; it gets on my nerves – es ärgert mich; to be ace – supertoll sein

"I don't," he confessed. "Other than that they eat, go for pees, and bark."

"Exactly," I nodded. And I **resolved** to buy a book about dogs in case there was something else that you had to know. Then I'd be able to give him a tip or two for dealing with dogs. That would certainly impress him.

"If you want, I can teach you something about dogs," I offered.

"What?" he asked, interested.

"Ah, that's a science in itself," I played it down. "I'll tell you a bit about it tomorrow." First I had to buy the book.

"Are you coming again tomorrow?" he asked, pleased.

I went red yet again. "I go for a walk every day. So I can go walking with you and Herr Schmitt, too. What sorts of things do you want to know about dogs?"

"Well, how you teach them tricks, for example. And how they learn **to walk to heel**."

Okay, so I'll have to **learn** this chapter **off by heart**. Ridiculous, in fact – God knows, I've got enough to do for school, and now I've got to study a book on dogs as well. But whatever. The things you do!

---

to resolve – sich entschließen;
to walk to heel – bei Fuß laufen;
to learn sth off by heart – etw. auswendig lernen

I nodded generously. "I'll explain it all to you tomorrow."

"Okay," he said. Then he looked at the time. "I've got to take Herr Schmitt home. Until tomorrow, then."

"Until tomorrow," I said, and my heart beat faster. Easy or what? I couldn't get my mind round it: I'd already got a second date with the coolest guy in town!

Lucilla won't believe it.

Friday 20th October

Lucilla could hardly believe it.

"Just like that? You met him in the middle of town and he asked you to go for a walk with him?"

"Yes," I replied casually, as if it were nothing special. I left out the business about the dog. To my mind, the story sounded even more exciting without the dog. And, of course, I didn't mention anything about the loo paper either – that was just too embarrassing.

"And he's sixteen?" Lucilla couldn't get her head round it. "I can't believe your luck!"

"Well…," I said modestly. "No, I don't know how I manage it either."

In the depths of my heart, I knew exactly how I

managed it. Something totally embarrassing happens; I get into a complete panic and try to **salvage** whatever is salvageable. And by doing so, I mostly make things even worse than they already are – but on occasion, something does actually work out.

"Jojo's new boyfriend is sixteen," Lucilla informed Carla as she approached us.

I gave Lucilla a dirty look. Shocked, she clapped her hand to her mouth. "Argh! Oh, I'm sorry, Jojo, I forgot I wasn't supposed to say anything. But it's so totally exciting, and I didn't mean any harm."

I nodded generously. Lucilla never really meant any harm.

"And Carla definitely won't spread it around. Will you, Carla?"

"Of course not," said Carla, immediately looking innocent.

Lucilla took that as an invitation to tell Carla every single detail of my love life. "They meet every day," Lucilla put Carla in the picture. "And he's totally sweet. The coolest guy in town. And he's sixteen!"

"You already told me that," Carla informed the excited Lucilla.

But that made no impression on Lucilla. She rolled her eyes in rapture and repeated again: "Sixteen! And he's mad about our Jojo." As if it **enhanced** her own and Carla's status.

---

to salvage – retten; to enhance – steigern

Carla seemed to be impressed. But she's always a bit jealous, and then she likes to look for **flaws** in other people's idylls. She thought for a moment, then asked with a **malicious** smirk: "Have you kissed yet?"

"Of course they haven't kissed yet. You don't start kissing the moment you meet someone," Lucilla **reproached** her. Then she looked at me, slightly shocked. "Or do you?"

"No," I confirmed.

Lucilla seemed relieved. Then she turned to Carla again. "Otherwise Jojo would have told me that ages ago." Carla nodded; that seemed plausible.

I did actually find Lucilla much nicer than Carla. Especially when Carla asked: "And where might we be able to get a look at this dream guy?"

"He's at the Humboldt," I said abruptly.

"No, not at school. We could just happen to be walking past when you meet him," Carla suggested.

Lucilla's eyes shone. "Oh, yes, please, Jojo. I absolutely have to see him."

"What's he called?" asked Carla.

But this was all getting way too much for me. "Oh, stop bombarding me with so many questions!"

"Come on, you could tell us his name," Lucilla said.

---

flaw – Makel, Fehler; malicious – böswillig;
to reproach – vorwerfen

I had to think. That name business was already a bit awkward. I couldn't tell the truth. Eberhard: that just didn't sound like a totally gorgeous guy. I needed a seriously cool name. Hmm. What about Sven? Sven sounds good. Yes, very good. And it's one of my favourite boy's names.

I decided to call him Sven. The only problem is: Eberhard doesn't know that he's called Sven. So I had to make sure that the pair of them didn't start chatting to him and call him Sven. Or I'll forget about the whole thing.

On the other hand, I really wanted to **show** Eberhard **off**. He looked so cool. The pair of them would definitely be blown away, right on the spot.

"What's the matter now?" **pestered** Carla.

"Slowly," I **grumbled**. "Let's take things one at a time. So: he's called Sven. And if you happen to be in the park during the afternoons, you can see him. See us. We always go for a walk there. Every day."

"We'll **lie in wait** this afternoon," giggled Lucilla.

"But do me a favour, and don't come and chat to me. You can look at him, but not talk to him. Okay?"

No reaction.

"Okay?" I demanded.

---

to show sb off – jmdn. vorführen;
to pester – nerven, bedrängen; to grumble – murren;
to lie in wait for sb – jmdm. auflauern

Carla gave me a mistrustful look. "Why can't we speak to him?"

Lucilla **tugged** at Carla's arm. "Don't make such a fuss! Seeing him is enough, isn't it?"

I was eternally grateful to Lucilla. She really is a good friend.

Friday evening, 20th October

On my way to meet Eberhard this afternoon, I was even more **worked up** than usual, because Carla and Lucilla were going to appear.

If only I'd kept my **trap** shut! But there are some things that you just have to tell people. And this applies above all to anything to do with love. It simply is more fun to be in love if your girlfriend knows about it.

Anyway, it was much too late now.

Eberhard came towards me, beaming, and gave me a package.

I went **beetroot** red. "For me?"

"Open it!" he said.

Oh wow, it was a present. He's brought me a pre-

---

to tug – zupfen, zerren; to be worked up – aufgeregt sein; trap (slang) – Gosche/Maul; beetroot – Rote Bete sent! I was completely **gobsmacked**. And I instantly felt terribly embarrassed because I hadn't come armed with a present for him. I'd have to think up a good excuse for that one! Totally thrilled, I unwrapped the package.

And what was in it? Dog biscuits!

Seriously, this is the honest truth: dog biscuits.

I didn't get it at first, and presumably looked a bit blank. He saw that he was forced to explain his present.

"They're dog biscuits!" he said cheerfully.

I nodded. "So I see."

"Well?" he asked expectantly.

"I can honestly say," I said hesitantly, "I'm not so keen on dog biscuits."

His eyes widened. I thought: now I've disappointed him terribly, and I was already wondering whether I couldn't possibly take a bite after all, and pretend that I really liked them, when he said: "But they're not for you."

That confused me even more.

"They're for Herr Schmitt," he said.

"And am I supposed to unwrap them for him?" I guessed cautiously.

"Um… you're the dog expert, aren't you? If you want to teach dogs something, you have to give them a reward. So I thought: I'll bring you some dog biscuits, and you can teach Herr Schmitt to do tricks."

---

gobsmacked – sprachlos, verdattert

"Oh, yeah, right. I knew that," I said, somewhat disappointed. But what could I really expect? Why should he bring me a present?!

As I turned down the path towards the park, he said: "Listen, let's walk across the field. Then we can let Herr Schmitt off the lead and give him a run. Okay?"

"Okay," I said.

It was all fine by me. The main thing was that Eberhard was walking next to me.

He was so sweet! I **reckon** he's really interested in me. Not just because he spends his spare time with me, but – ha – because he then asked me if I had a boyfriend. Just like that, **out of the blue**.

Herr Schmitt had just gone running off all over the place, when he suddenly asked: "Hey, have you got a boyfriend?"

Well, how about that? If that's not a proposition, I don't know what it is!

"No-o-o," I immediately replied, keen to eliminate all doubt.

Thank goodness I wasn't still with Nils. I thought Nils was really nice and stuff, but … I don't know. Somehow he just didn't give me **butterflies in my tummy**.

---

to reckon – glauben; out of the blue – aus heiterem Himmel; butterflies in my tummy – Bauchkribbeln, Schmetterlinge im Bauch

Butterflies in my tummy? What kind of expression is that? The thought of having 'butterflies' in your tummy is totally revolting. Honestly. I mean, how would they get in there? As **caterpillars**? Bleurgh. No-o-o, really, that's a stupid expression.

Now, all that stuff about hearing a thousand violins playing is better. You know: you're supposed to hear a thousand violins playing when you kiss the man of your dreams. Though I have to admit that I'd be surprised if I suddenly heard violins and there wasn't a radio on somewhere. I'd be straight off to the doctor's.

Ah well, whatever. Back then, with Nils, it just wasn't that kind of hundred percent exciting. I mean, he was really nice and all that. He was really good looking and stuff. But somehow… I probably just wasn't sufficiently in love with him.

No chance.

But being in love isn't that simple. Not in my case, at any rate. Being in love has to happen differently somehow.

With a bang. You have to fall in love without warning. You see someone, and you're blown away. The guy has to be a knockout. Just like Eberhard.

And if Eberhard isn't a knockout, then I don't know… At any rate, I did immediately **fall head-**

---

caterpillar – Raupe; to fall head-over-heels in front of sb – vor jmdm. eine Bauchlandung machen

over-heels in front of him the first time I saw him. That was a sign – it's obvious.

But if you think that falling in love is some kind of skill, it's got nothing on finishing with someone. Phew! Honestly.

For me, telling Nils that we should finish was really stressful.

At first I just wanted to avoid doing it. I thought Nils would work out what the matter was if I simply **steered clear of** him for long enough.

But it didn't work.

It did at first, but then he just **accosted** me and wanted to know what was wrong.

"Nothing," I said.

"I thought, because you were avoiding me…"

"Me? Really? Nah!" That was mega-stupid. Why did I say that? Nils was right, for goodness' sake! But it was already too late.

So Nils then said, quite cheerfully: "Good, let's go to the cinema then."

"Good idea," I lied, and went to the cinema with him.

Great way to finish with someone. Especially because you normally go to the cinema for a **snog**. And snogging with someone is doubtless not the most inspired way of finishing with them.

---

to steer clear of sb – jmdm. aus dem Weg gehen;
to accost sb – jmdn. ansprechen; snog (slang) – Kussorgie

So, I thought, all I have to do is make sure that Nils doesn't kiss me. Then everything would be fine.

But in fact it was **foul**. I thought I was as **cunning** as cunning could be, and that I just had to make sure that I was constantly eating. Because you can't kiss with your mouth full. It worked, too.

But by the end, I thought I was going to be violently sick. And when I told Nils, all he said was: "No wonder you feel sick – you've been stuffing yourself the whole time."

I nodded, feeling ill, and said I wanted to go home now.

He took me home and said: "Okay, see you tomorrow." So that didn't help me.

Well, anyway, the whole thing dragged on for a couple more days, and I behaved pretty stupidly. So stupidly that eventually Nils said: "Listen, is it that you don't want to see me any more?"

It was my big chance. And what did I say?

"No-o-o-o, absolutely not. What gives you that idea?" That's how stupid I was.

Whereupon, Nils said: "Hmmm, but to be honest, *I* don't want to carry on. You're behaving pretty stupidly."

My eyes widened and I asked: "What's that supposed to mean?"

---

foul – furchtbar; cunning – schlau

Nils took a deep breath and said: "I don't think we should see each other any more."

I was totally gobsmacked. So that's how it worked. He made it pretty easy for himself. To be honest, I was pretty indignant.

Very **primly** and pointedly, I then said: "Oh, is that supposed to mean you're finishing with me?"

Nils was a bit embarrassed, and **mumbled**: "Well, um, you know, you're kind of not particularly nice to me any more."

"Oh, so that's the reason why you don't want to see me any more? Thanks, that's fine by me," I said **pertly**, before turning and walking off.

Ah well, so that's how it was.

A couple of days later I apologized to him and said that he had been right and that I wasn't **cross** or anything.

And now everything's just as it was before. Well, not quite. I still find the whole business a bit embarrassing, so I try to avoid running into Nils.

But it was a really big shock to discover that finishing with someone is an art that you have to learn. In my case, at any rate. I don't seem to have a natural talent for it. Just like falling in love.

---

prim – formell, steif; to mumble – nuscheln;
pert – schnippisch, keck; to be cross – sauer sein

I'd never finish with Eberhard.

He is just so-o-o-o-o-o-o fantastic.

I impressed him with my superb knowledge and abilities regarding dog training. At least I tried. After all, I had studied a book on dogs.

When he asked me about my boyfriend and I said I didn't have one, I was so embarrassed that I immediately started issuing commands to Herr Schmitt.

"Here, Herr Schmitt. Here! Sit. *Sit!*" But Herr Schmitt didn't respond. He didn't pay the slightest attention to my commands. Not even when I waved the dog biscuits around. The dog obviously couldn't see very well. He ran over the fields **panting** and barking, and I was glad nobody was around, because Herr Schmitt made a pretty stupid impression.

I called again. "Here, Herr Schmitt, Herr Schmitt, *here*. **Heel**!"

I was starting to seriously worry about whether the dog might perhaps have hearing damage when Eberhard gave a short whistle, and Herr Schmitt immediately came running up.

I quickly gave Herr Schmitt a dog biscuit and said to Eberhard: "See, that's how easy it is. When they do as they're told, you have to give them a reward. They realise what's happening, and the next time, they do it again. You just don't use the same commands every time. He obviously reacted to 'heel'.

---

to pant – hecheln; Heel! – Bei Fuß!

So we have to remember that. Good boy, Herr Schmitt," I praised the dog, as if he had actually obeyed my **hoarse** shouting.

Eberhard smiled at me and said: "You're really sweet." And I **fainted**. Well, almost. Not really. I fainted inside, because that was undoubtedly an **unambiguous** declaration of love – wasn't it?!

"You, too," I said, and could then have bitten my tongue out. How stupid of me! "You, too" – how pathetically stupid. Boys aren't sweet. Well, of course they're sweet, but you don't tell them that.

"Um, I mean, you're really ..." I almost said 'cool', but that seemed to me not to be so inspired after all, so I said 'nice'.

Then I was annoyed with myself for having said something so **mundane** as 'nice'. And I also started to feel annoyed with myself for being so crazy about him, because I always talk nonsense when I'm in love with someone. Who organised the world to make that happen? That's precisely when you need to be at your most brilliant, quick-witted and super-intelligent.

"Are you coming again tomorrow?" Eberhard asked me.

I merely nodded, for fear of saying something else stupid.

---

hoarse – heiser; to faint – in Ohnmacht fallen;
unambiguous – eindeutig; mundane – profan

"Okay, till tomorrow, little angel." He said little angel. I sighed.

Once I was alone and making my way home again, I suddenly felt boiling hot when it struck me that Lucilla and Carla would have been waiting in the park **in vain** today. Yet another stupid thing. They'll definitely be annoyed. Oh, so what. What do Lucilla and Carla matter to me if I have Eberhard and Herr Schmitt? Herr Schmitt? Rubbish – if I have Eberhard.

What a dreamy afternoon.

When I got home, my mother said: "You look like a wet dog! Didn't you notice that it was raining?"

"Raining?" I asked, still thinking loving thoughts about Eberhard. "Nah."

"Jojo, darling, do I have to start worrying about you yet again?" my mother asked anxiously.

"About me?"

"Yes, about you!"

I **hugged** her, sopping wet as I was, and said: "I feel wonderful!" Then I disappeared into my room.

"What about food?" my mother shouted through the door.

"Not hungry!" I shouted back.

Then I heard my mother sighing, and quietly saying: "Here we go again. Jojo's smitten."

---

in vain – umsonst; to hug sb – jmdn. umarmen

"I saw Jojo walking across the field with a camel yesterday," declared Flippi over breakfast this morning.

My mother looked at me. "Jojo, is that true?"

"Not a word of it!" I defended myself, immediately indignant.

"With a camel?" my mother asked Flippi.

I just don't believe it. I said quite clearly it wasn't true, and she just carries on quite **unconcerned,** talking to her favourite daughter.

Flippi nodded vigorously. "One hump on its back, and another on its head. Someone's **palmed** a deformed camel **off on** Jojo."

This family is going to drive me mad!

"It was an Emperor Poodle!"

"There are Emperor Penguins. Might it have been a penguin?" suggested my mother helpfully.

I rolled my eyes. "Oh wow, you're really getting on my nerves."

"Well, I have to say I find it all a bit **disconcerting**, Josefine. What's this story all about? Tell me a bit at a time."

"Let Flippi tell you. She always knows better, anyway," I **grouched**, and **shrouded** myself in silence.

---

unconcerned – gleichgültig; to palm sth off on sb – jmdm. etwas aufhalsen; disconcerting – beunruhigend; to grouch – motzen; to shroud – einhüllen

My mother looked expectantly at Flippi.

Flippi smirked. "I think it's because of the new hair colour. The dye obviously got into Jojo's brain and destroyed her brain cells. That is to say, the couple of cells that were still working."

"Flippi!" my mother **reprimanded** her, turning to me in a **conciliatory** way. "Do I have to worry about you, darling?"

There it was again: 'darling'. When will she finally stop saying that?

I gave my mother another chance. "I took my friend's grandmother's dog for a walk with him."

"Oh, a dog," cried my mother, relieved. "So why did you say it was a penguin?"

I was in despair. "I didn't say it was a penguin. You said that. Emperor Penguin. But it was an Emperor Poodle. A dog."

"You mean a King Poodle!" cried my mother, relieved.

How embarrassing: of course it was a King Poodle. What made me say Emperor? Ah well.

"Exactly," I said, and that was the end of the matter so far as I was concerned.

"He's definitely **descended from** a camel," cried Flippi.

"That's not very polite of you, Fillipine!" my

---

to reprimand – rügen; conciliatory – versöhnlich;
to descend from – abstammen von

mother reprimanded Flippi. "If he's a friend of Jojo's, he's bound to be nice."

"I meant the dog," explained Flippi. "But strictly speaking, you're right, Mum. There's definitely something wrong with Jojo's friend too. Who in the entire world would keep a deformed camel and call it a poodle? He must be **off his rocker**."

Flippi was in high spirits. I absolutely had to change the topic, or she'd never stop going on about it.

"Mum, how are you getting on with the dress for *The Marriage of Figaro*?"

"It's ready," beamed my mother. A brilliant diversion. My mother loves it when people are interested in her job.

I wanted to play safe and make sure the poodle topic had been forgotten once and for all. "Can I see it?"

"No!" cried Flippi. My mother and I gave each other astonished looks. What was all that about? There had to be a reason behind it.

"Have you done something to the costume?" I asked Flippi, just **on the off chance**.

Flippi's eyes **blazed** with anger, and my mother looked terrified. "What's happened to the costume?" she cried shrilly, then jumped up and ran off to fetch it.

---

to be off one's rocker – verrückt sein;
on the off chance – für den Fall; to blaze – feurig strahlen

My mother is, you see, a costume designer for the theatre. That means she designs and cuts out costumes for theatre productions. She mostly works at home so she can be with the 'children'. More than half the time, she curses this decision because it means that not only she but also her costumes are with the 'children'. And in Flippi's case (and she's the only one we're talking about here when we use the word 'children'), that means my mother's creations are **in mortal danger**. Because Flippi spends her life experimenting with them. With things that are expensive, unique and irreplaceable.

"**Prat**!" hissed Flippi to me.

I shrugged my shoulders. "Sorry, I couldn't have known…"

Our mother returned with the costume over her arm. Blank horror stood in her eyes. What had once been pure white silk now looked as if an angry old hippy had been sleeping in it.

The costume was ruined. Now Flippi was in for it. My mother would **tar and feather** her.

"Flippi!" cried my mother, barely able to control herself.

Tar, feather, and run her out of town – that's what my mother would do to her. Things didn't look too good for Little Miss Don't-Blame-Me.

---

in mortal danger – in Lebensgefahr; Prat! (vulgär) – Arschloch!; to tar and feather sb – jmdn. teeren und federn

"What happened to this?" cried my mother.

"Don't get worked up, Mummy. It was an accident. Honest."

"I'll decide whether it was an accident or not. Tell me at once what happened!" My mother's voice was very sharp.

Flippi adopted her totally **remorseful** 'I'm-still-very-small-really-and-don't-ever-mean-any-harm' expression and began to tell her story hesitantly, with tiny **sobs** in her voice. "We were supposed to take a piece of white fabric to school for Textile Design, because we're doing batik at the moment. And you weren't there, and I couldn't ask you. But I had to take something white with me, and I just..." At this point, Flippi's voice broke most effectively, and she just sobbed.

"I thought... because... you're not so keen on marriages and stuff... and I was sure you didn't need the dress any more... and so I just..."

Obviously Flippi suddenly had an idea.

She stopped sobbing, looked **ingenuously** at my mother, and said proudly: "I got an A for it. The teacher thought it was fantastic."

My mother didn't respond.

Whereupon Flippi started **bawling**. "And I thought you'd be proud of me. You always want me

---

remorseful – reumütig; sob – Schluchzer;
ingenuous – unschuldig; to bawl – flennen

to get good marks and stuff… and now everything's so awful. I know you hate me now."

Oh, that was good. Flippi was on top form.

My mother's eyes turned mild and pitying, and she took her favourite daughter in her arms and comforted her.

I felt sick. She was comforting the child. I couldn't believe it.

"Now stop crying, sweetheart. Of course I don't hate you. But it will take a lot of work to put that dress right…" She looked at the dress and corrected herself. "…To **re-stitch** it."

As she did start to sound annoyed again, Flippi started **howling** even more loudly. "I'm always making so much work for you. I'm a dreadful child. You really shouldn't love me any more."

My mother sighed. "Don't worry about it, sweetheart. It's not that much work."

"Yes it is," cried Flippi **defiantly**.

My mother was in despair. "No, it's not. I like doing it. Strictly speaking, the dress wasn't that good anyway. I really wanted **to start from scratch**."

Flippi beamed. "Then you were lucky that I took it to batik."

My mother frowned, irritated. "I wouldn't say

---

to re-stitch sth – etw. noch mal nähen;
to howl – heulen; defiant – trotzig;
to start from scratch – von vorne anfangen

that exactly. But let's close the subject. Not another word about it."

Flippi **wiped** the tears from her face and gave me a triumphant look.

She's good, plain and simple. She's better. Better than all of us put together.

Monday 23rd October

Lucilla and Carla complained bitterly at school this morning.

"We spent the whole boring Friday afternoon hanging around the park, and who didn't appear? Your ominous boyfriend Sven, and our dear Jojo," Carla snapped at me.

Even my best friend Lucilla had kind of worry lines on her face. "I mean, honestly. That really was kind of stupid, Jojo," she said, adding her bit to Carla's **gripe**.

"What was I supposed to do? Sven wanted to walk across the fields instead. Because of Herr Schmitt."

"Herr Schmitt?"

Oh damn, I'd totally forgotten that I hadn't so much as mentioned Herr Schmitt yet.

"Who's Herr Schmitt?"

---

to wipe – wischen; gripe – Meckerei

Was I supposed to say 'a dog?' No way, that simply didn't sound good.

"His Maths teacher."

"Eh?"

Oh, that probably wasn't so great after all.

"His Maths teacher goes jogging in the park, and Sven didn't want to **bump into** him."

"See?" said Lucilla triumphantly to Carla. "I just told you there **was bound** to be a reason."

"Huh," snorted Carla.

"He'll definitely be in the park this afternoon. Guaranteed," I immediately offered in order to **appease** Carla. Then I felt annoyed again. Why was I making such an effort to please these idiots?!

Ah well, if they want to have a look at Eberhard, it can't do any harm. Then that'll put an end to the topic once and for all. Then we're finished, and I can be left in peace.

Monday evening, 23rd October

Eberhard was so-o-o-o sweet this afternoon. He arrived with a package again and gave it to me.

"Dog biscuits?" I asked.

---

to bump into sb – jmdn. zufällig treffen; to be bound – auf jeden Fall; to appease – beruhigen, besänftigen

He shook his head. "Go on, unwrap it!"

I unwrapped it, and saw a nougat ring.

"A nougat ring?" I asked cautiously, my hopes already starting to rise.

Eberhard grinned. "It's for you. You were a bit disappointed last time because of the dog biscuits, weren't you?"

"Nah, not in the slightest," I lied. But then I beamed gratefully and bit straight into it.

"Tastes fantastic, thanks."

"You're very welcome," he said, laughing.

"Do you want a bite?" I offered.

Oh, where on earth were Lucilla and Carla? Now would be the ideal moment. They had to see me now. See us. Then they'd be seriously impressed. Eberhard looked totally gorgeous. Almost better than ever. And he was taking a bite of my nougat ring. You couldn't be more in love than that.

I was in seventh heaven.

But Eberhard was somehow not in a terribly good mood. I wanted to cheer him up, and said: "I think it's so brilliant of you to do this for your grandmother! Shall I take Herr Schmitt's lead?"

He nodded. Then he looked straight ahead of him anxiously.

"What's the matter?" I asked sympathetically.

"Oh, I feel really bad."

"Why? I like holding Herr Schmitt's lead."

"No, I don't mean that." He looked me in the face.

I grabbed hold of my hair. "It's okay about the platinum blonde, I've always wanted to dye my hair."

He frowned, as if he thought I was a bit **daft**. "It's because of my grandmother. I take her dog out every day. And she's so pleased about it."

I nodded. "But that's fantastic."

And I *was* pleased, too. For his grandmother and for myself.

"Yes," he said, again looking anxiously at the ground. "And I'd like to carry on doing it, if only the business about sorting out the homework in the children's home hadn't come up."

"Sorting out the homework?"

"I offered to help the kids at the children's home with their homework. Doing a good **deed**, and all that. I reckon everyone should do their bit for the common good."

Wow, I was just **dumbfounded**. He's good looking, charming, and a good person. That really is just too good to be true.

"I think that's brilliant of you. Honestly."

He nodded. Then he looked strained again and sighed loudly.

"What's the matter?" I asked.

He looked at me a bit annoyed. "Oh, I just told you: my grandmother and Herr Schmitt."

---

daft – bekloppt; deed – Tat;
dumbfounded – sprachlos, verblüfft

“What’s wrong with them?”

He began to lose patience with me. “I take the dog out every day, but I can’t do it any more because of the kids in the home.”

Oh, right, of course. I really wasn’t with it. Either that, or I was just too much in love to concentrate on what he was saying.

I thought hard. Now I had to impress him somehow. With a totally brilliant solution.

I began cautiously. “Perhaps I can help you somehow?” I offered.

He beamed charmingly, excitedly, in love with me. “Would you really do that?”

I was slightly baffled by his **effusive** response. All I said was that I might be able to help him.

“I think that’s totally fantastic of you. The first time I saw you, I knew you were the type. I knew at once that you were… an… an…”

“Angel,” I helped him out. Pity he kept forgetting. “You said I looked like an angel,” I **persisted**, slightly annoyed.

He nodded. “Yes, of course, an angel. Thanks a million, that really is totally lovely of you. But if you’re going to help me out, you must let me invite you for an ice-cream or to the cinema or something.”

I went beetroot red and shrugged my shoulders,

---

effusive – überschwänglich; to persist – beharren

slightly embarrassed. "If you like. That'd be fine by me." That did not, of course, correspond to my true feelings. But I thought: it's a whole lot cooler than throwing myself round his neck with joy and shouting: "Yes, yes, yes! Thanks! Thanks a million!"

He turned quite businesslike. "Okay, why don't we start today?"

"What with?"

"With you taking Herr Schmitt out on your own."

"I'm taking Herr Schmitt out on my own?" I asked, puzzled.

"But you said so yourself!" he said **reproachfully**.

What? So when did that happen? I wanted to go and have an ice-cream with Eberhard, to go to the cinema with him, not to take his weird mutt for a walk.

He looked at me with big eyes. **Boundless** disappointment spread across his face. "Oh, so that's how it is," he said, **offended**. "You don't want to help me after all."

I couldn't allow that. After all, he was a good person and I was an angel!

"I'll do it!" I cried. "Just tell me why again."

He smiled again. "Because I can't **simultaneously** take the dog out and sort out the homework," he

---

reproachful – vorwurfsvoll; boundless – grenzenlos;
to offend sb – jmdn. beleidigen; simultaneous – gleichzeitig

explained to me with the **utmost** patience, almost as if he were talking to someone with a pea for a brain.

Now I felt pretty stupid. So that's what he'd been talking about the whole time! "Oh, yeah, of course." I hesitated. Then I did ask: "Just… um, please don't be cross or anything… but why am I supposed to start today? Do you have to go to the children's home already?"

He somehow lost the thread, and then said: "No, not until tomorrow. But we should check – test so to speak – whether it works. You and Herr Schmitt alone. Whether it all works out okay."

"Oh, right." I nodded. That made some sort of sense.

"So: you walk round the park with Herr Schmitt for an hour, and then we'll meet here again."

I looked at him, baffled.

"Don't you want to?" he asked, disappointed.

"Oh yes, of course I'd love to!" I cried quickly, because I couldn't bear seeing him with such sad eyes.

And so I ended up taking Herr Schmitt for a pee. On my own. At first I was a bit annoyed, but the longer I thought about it, the more fantastic I started to think it was. It was a genuine proof of trust. He really must like me quite a lot. Yes, the way to a boy's heart is sometimes through his dog-lead. Or something like that.

---

utmost – äußerst

However, what was totally stupid was that I did then meet Lucilla and Carla. Duh! It would have to happen like that. The idiots only appeared once Eberhard was miles away and I was completely alone, walking through the park with the Bengal tiger.

When I saw the pair of them, I immediately did an about-turn, but it was already too late. They came running after me.

"Hey, wait up, Jojo!" called Lucilla.

I had no alternative. I turned and acted as if I had only just seen them.

"Oh, hello. What are you doing here?"

"Didn't you see us, then?" asked Carla suspiciously.

"Nah, not at all."

"What kind of dog is *that*?" asked Lucilla, mildly horrified.

"What dog?" I attempted to act dumb.

"That one you've got on a lead," explained Lucilla.

"Oh, that one!" I **feigned** surprise. "That's…"

'Herr Schmitt' was what I really didn't want to say now. That was already the name of Eberhard's Maths teacher.

"… It's our neighbour's dog. She's ill, so I'm taking him for a walk. Doing a good deed, and all that."

Lucilla nodded. "I thought you were going to meet Sven."

I didn't speak for a moment, as I firstly had to re-

---

to feign – vortäuschen

cover from the embarrassment of them having caught me with Herr Schmitt.

And the **impertinent** Carla took advantage of my silence to point to the dog and ask **smugly**: "Or might that be Sven?" She started to laugh unpleasantly.

Then she bent down to Herr Schmitt and spoke to him in a baby voice. "So, so, you're Sven, then. Sixteen years old. A totally cool guy. No wonder Jojo's so crazy about you."

Lucilla couldn't resist giggling, and then the two idiots stood there almost dying of laughter. I wanted to die, it was so embarrassing. But then I gave Lucilla a somewhat angry look. That often does the trick.

Lucilla immediately stopped laughing. "Sorry, Jojo, but it's just too funny…" And then she started laughing again.

So I turned on my heel and went home. That really did go seriously wrong!

Tuesday 24th October

"Are you still annoyed with me?" Lucilla **besieged** me this morning at school.

"No-o-o," I growled.

---

impertinent – frech; smug – selbstgefällig;
to besiege – belagern, bedrängen

"I have never doubted for a single moment that your Sven exists. Honestly. Carla was just so funny. The way she talked to the dog! That's why I laughed."

"It doesn't matter," I graciously forgave Lucilla.

Whereupon she immediately asked: "Can I come and look again today?"

I **pondered**. It would be difficult to catch the right moment. Eberhard just wanted to hand Herr Schmitt over to me quickly and then collect him again later. It would be really stupid if she were to see me just with the dog instead of with Eberhard.

"I'll come on my own, if you like," offered Lucilla.

Damn, what should I do?

"I don't know yet if I'll have time," I said cautiously.

Lucilla looked startled. "Is everything okay with you two?"

"Of course," I snapped at her.

What gave her an idea like that?

"It's best if I ring you and tell you when I'm meeting him. Okay?" I suggested.

"Woof woof!" suddenly came from behind me.

Carla. Oh great!

I made sure I got the hell out of it, and scarpered.

---

to ponder – tief nachdenken

All afternoon, I was totally neurotic, because I was constantly thinking that Lucilla or Carla were **lurking** behind every tree. I really was all **uptight**, and in a bad mood.

That may perhaps also be due to the fact that Eberhard wasn't going for walks with me any more. I walked around on my own, and found it pretty **dismal**.

In the end, I tried to concentrate on the fact that I'd soon hand Herr Schmitt over and then I'd see Eberhard again.

But Eberhard immediately rushed off because Herr Schmitt urgently needed his dinner. So yet again: nothing. Stupid Herr Schmitt.

But so what: at least Eberhard and I do see each other, and at some point he might have time for me too.

You just have to be patient. And it's worth it for a guy like Eberhard.

My mother, of course, immediately had to pass comment on this new development. "If you really like doing it, okay. But don't let this young man **take advantage of** you."

Take advantage? Pah. He'd never do that. What's more, it was my idea.

---

to lurk – lauern; uptight – nervös, angespannt; dismal – öde; to take advantage of sb – jmdn. ausnutzen

Or that's what I think, at any rate.

I shouldn't have told my mother anything about it. But somehow I never manage to keep my trap shut with my own mother – I just have to **blurt** everything **out**.

Wednesday 25th October

Flippi is a serious pain. But what else can you expect from someone who **breeds slugs**? I mean, normal little sisters collect Barbies, swap stickers or, as far as I know, even collect stamps. But slugs? Ugh.

When she was passing today, Flippi sniffed and said: "My goodness, you smell of dog again!"

"And you smell of slug," I **countered**.

"Dog is worse!"

"It's nothing to do with you. Keep your distance," I said shortly.

"Couldn't you at least have found someone who had a normal looking mutt?"

"Leave me alone, pratface!"

Flippi shrugged her shoulders. "It won't last anyway."

---

to blurt sth out – mit etw. herausplatzen, etw. ausschwatzen;
to breed – züchten; slug – Nacktschnecke;
to counter – kontern, erwidern

"Eh? What makes you think that?"

"Do you wanna **bet**?"

"Bet what?"

"Bet the whole thing will end soon?"

"Bet it won't!?"

"Bet it will!?"

Now, though, I was becoming annoyed. "What are you on about?"

Flippi smirked. "Your journey will soon be pretty long."

"Eh?"

Flippi smirked even more broadly. "Well, I doubt that your beloved will have you flown in to take the dog out."

"What kind of **drivel** is this?"

Flippi feigned astonishment. "Don't say you don't know yet."

"What?"

Flippi looked even more astonished. "Oh, obviously not. Um, then forget what I said." And she made as if to disappear.

I grabbed hold of her collar and demanded threateningly: "Tell me now what's wrong!"

Flippi put on a frightened expression and with feigned **concern**, she said: "Mum might have forgotten to tell you, but *we're* ***moving house***."

---

to bet – wetten; drivel – Unsinn; concern – Besorgnis; to move house – umziehen

"What?" I've never moved house in my entire life. And I'm certainly not about to start now. Now, when my love life is just running at full speed and everything is so perfect. "Where to?"

Flippi smirked again. "A long way away. You'll have to say goodbye to the dog-camel."

"Where?"

"To London."

"London? In England?"

"That's where it was when I last looked at the atlas, at any rate," Flippi said pertly.

"We're moving to England? Why don't I know anything about it?"

"Perhaps because your head is full of nothing but this mutt, um, I mean this guy. We..."

"M-u-u-u-um..." I released Flippi and ran to my mother.

My mother was in her work room, working on the ruined wedding costume, and had her mouth full of pins when I stormed in.

"Why didn't I know about it?"

My mother was startled and **spat** the pins out in a panic. "My God, Jojo. What's all that about? Do you have to **startle** me like that? I almost swallowed the pins."

She began to count the pins she had spat out. "It's possible that I did swallow one. Honestly."

---

to spit – spucken; to startle – erschrecken

My mother will drive me mad. I felt like crying. "Why are we moving to London?" I sobbed.

"Oh, nothing's decided for certain yet. I've had an offer. The director of the London theatre, who gave a guest performance here, asked me if I'd like to work for him."

"Don't they have costume designers in England? Why you of all people?"

My mother was slightly indignant. "Hey, Jojo, you could be pleased for me. It's a huge compliment, anyway. When they were here, I stepped in for their costume designer. You must still remember that. He got mumps."

I shook my head.

My mother sighed. "Here we go again. You really are only interested in your own life. You don't take in what happens around you."

"That's normal for a teenager," I told her. Because I had **flicked through** my mother's parenting manuals and advice tomes too.

"Whatever. In any case, the director was so taken by my work that he offered me the chance to work for him."

"Why didn't you say anything to me?" I grumbled.

"I mentioned it over supper two days ago. Quite apart from that, nothing is decided. It's just an offer

---

to flick through – durchblättern

at present. Something like that requires a lot of consideration."

"Something like that doesn't need any consideration at all. We're not accepting the offer. **Reject** him, or my entire life is ruined," I ordered, and left the room.

"It's my life too, you know!" my mother called after me.

I couldn't get my mind round it. How could she be so egoistical! The very woman who only ever has her eye on the well-being of her children; who'll do anything to make her children happy. And so she ruins not only our lives, our mood, and our whole belief in motherhood, but sometimes gives us a guilty conscience as well because she never thinks about herself.

Now at her ripe old age, she suddenly wants to do something that she enjoys?! She can't suddenly change the rules!

Well, Flippi and I have to take decisive action. Yes, Flippi and I. **When the chips are down**, we're a team.

---

to reject sb – jmdn. abweisen, absagen;
when the chips are down – wenn es hart auf hart kommt

Thursday 26th October

There's nothing to be done. Flippi wants to go to London. She thinks the slugs in London must be enormous because it rains so much there.

We'll be fighting in separate camps.

However, Flippi, like me, is opposed in principle to my mother suddenly starting to lead her own life. She's indignant. "Who put such stupid ideas into her head?"

But that doesn't help me any further. In any case, I have to go. I'm meeting Eberhard.

He promised to come slightly earlier today so we could spend a bit of time together.

Oh, he's so-o-o-o-o sweet. And so over-worked. Poor thing. I'm ever so glad that I can help him out with Herr Schmitt. I'd do anything for him.

And he's so grateful. He always beams at me really gratefully, and says: "That's so nice of you. I don't know what I'd do without you. You really are an angel."

When he says 'angel' to me, I melt on the spot. But I'd kind of like to tell him my name sometime. I mean, he doesn't know what I'm called. I do find that a bit annoying. He's never asked me. And I've never said anything either. And it's kind of stupid to tell him now, when we've known each other for a while. I can't really say out of the blue: "Oh, by the way, I'm called Jojo." That looks so pushy.

He just calls me angel. Which, of course, is much better. Because it sounds pretty much as if he's in love.

Nevertheless, I have to come up with a way of just dropping my name into the conversation.

Anyway, whatever, I really do think he's like the prince in a fairy-tale.

I'm entitled to it, too, after all the dramas I've had in my love life. The right man at last!

The thought of moving to London is truly awful. And it's not just for me. It would be totally dreadful for Eberhard, too. It would break his heart. Perhaps I shouldn't mention it until it's definite.

Thursday evening, 26th October

He didn't have any more time for me. He was late. He had to help his mother with the washing up. I should really have been cross.

But of course he has so little time only because he's such a totally nice and helpful guy. And I think that's fantastic.

So I forgave him. To make up for it, he wants to go to the cinema with me soon. About time, too, because why else am I making such a big fuss about the dog and stuff?

Anyway, I was **pootling**, or, rather, poodling **round** the park with Herr Schmitt, not thinking any particularly bad thoughts – when I suddenly had a terrible shock.

I had been looking at the ground the whole time, and hadn't noticed that anyone was approaching me. When I looked up, I was totally shocked: I was facing myself!

It was as if I were looking in a mirror. In front of me stood a girl who looked like me. My height, my figure, and… my hair colour. Platinum blonde.

We were both **taken aback**, then we had to laugh.

"Fantastic hair colour," said the girl, pointing to my head.

I nodded. "You too."

"Your dog looks like…" She searched for the right words.

I helped her out. "A blow-dried bodybuilder."

She almost laughed herself to death. "My name's Annette. How about you?"

"Jojo."

"Hello, Jojo."

"Hello, Annette."

She also had a dog with her, so we walked through the park together with our dogs, chatting.

She's so nice. She's taking her boyfriend's dog

---

to pootle around – umherschlendern;
to be taken aback – verblüfft sein

out. A **slobbery**, old, mud-brown bulldog. The dog. Not the boyfriend. Ugh, really disgusting. Wow, I was really lucky with Herr Schmitt. Herr Schmitt and I look a good deal better.

But the girl is really nice. She can't help her dog.

Isn't that a **coincidence**? Her taking her boyfriend's dog out for a walk, too. Just like me. We found that pretty amusing.

Her boyfriend is called Edgar. Definitely a bit better than Eberhard. I told her about Eberhard, but preferred to call him 'Sven' again. She thought he sounded pretty ace. I think she was a bit jealous because my boyfriend is called Sven and hers is just called Edgar.

The dog is called Mops. Can you believe it? Mops! How are you supposed to call him if he runs away? I mean, quite apart from the fact that it's anyway totally uncool to call 'Mops' out loud, 'Mops' isn't an easy name to shout. In fact, there's no good way of shouting 'Mops'. If you just shout 'Mops', it happens so quickly that the dog doesn't even notice it. So you have to call 'Mo-hops', which is totally ridiculous. I'd rather let the dog run away than call it. Honestly. 'Mo-hops'!" Nah, thanks.

Give me Herr Schmitt any day. If I had to call him, I wouldn't be embarrassed. People would think I'd seen my Maths teacher somewhere and

---

slobbery – sabbernd; coincidence – Zufall

was calling him. It would only be embarrassing if a dog ran up to you. But then I'd just put the dog on the lead and carry on calling 'Herr Schmitt', then no one would know that the dog was called Herr Schmitt.

Anyway. Annette just has to make sure that Mops doesn't run away.

Annette is in the class above me. At the same school. It's amazing how you keep meeting new people even though you should actually know each other. **By sight** and stuff.

We had a really lovely afternoon. It is actually extremely boring walking around on your own with a dog on a lead. In all weathers.

Anyway, Annette and I have arranged to meet every day now, and to go out as a **foursome** sometime. With Edgar and Eberhard, that is. Not with Herr Schmitt and Mops. For God's sake, we're *always* wandering around with them.

But Edgar, unfortunately, also has incredibly little time. Just like Eberhard. Oh well, guys are all the same.

Annette had to go before me, and I walked on for a bit on my own. Herr Schmitt **strained** terribly at his lead, and then something totally stupid happened:

---

by sight – vom Sehen; foursome – Vierergespann;
to strain – (hier:) zerren

Herr Schmitt spotted a rabbit, and ran off. Lead and all. It just slipped out of my hand.

I was in a total panic, because all I saw of the dog was a cloud of dust – and that was it. I chased through a whole load of bushes and shrubs – no luck. No trace of Herr Schmitt.

Then I saw a bush **wobbling** around like mad and barking every now and then. Something black and woolly was poking out from under the bush. No doubt about it: Herr Schmitt.

I really must have been pretty desperate, because with one **bound**, I **pounced upon** the bush and gripped tightly. I grabbed something woolly and dragged it out of the bush.

"Oh!" I yelled. "I've got you!"

"Would you mind letting me go?" asked the guy whose black woollen pullover I was clutching.

I was so embarrassed, I didn't have a clue what to say.

"The thing is, I've just caught a dog," said the guy, tugging on the lead. Herr Schmitt crept unwillingly out of the **undergrowth**. His rabbit-chasing had come to a premature end.

Grinning, the guy looked at his arm, which I was still clasping.

---

to wobble – schwanken, wackeln; bound – Sprung, Satz;
to pounce upon – sich stürzen auf;
undergrowth – Gebüsch, Gestrüpp

I followed his gaze, and immediately let go. "I'm so sorry, I thought... I didn't know," I stammered.

"Is that your dog?" he asked.

I nodded. Then I shook my head. "No-o-o, I'm just taking him for a walk." I finally found my voice again. "For an old lady," I added. That somehow sounded better than saying 'for a totally cool guy'. And strictly speaking, it was kind of true as well.

The guy laughed in a friendly manner.

My knees felt weak. Most likely because I'd been running so much.

"That really is a monster dog," he said, giving me the lead.

I took the lead, and pushed off with Herr Schmitt. Then something suddenly struck me. I turned round and almost ran straight into the guy, because he was running after me and was standing right behind me when I turned round.

We both had to laugh.

"I forgot to say thank you. It was really nice of you to catch Herr Schmitt," I said.

"Herr Schmitt?"

I nodded in the direction of the dog.

The guy laughed. "Herr Schmitt? Oh well, why not." Then he quickly looked at the ground as if he were gathering his courage together, before saying with a smile: "And I wanted to invite you for an ice-cream. Because of the shock and stuff ..."

I beamed. "Really? That's brilliant. I'd love to."

We went to the **ice-cream parlour** together. At first I was absolutely delighted. Then it occurred to me how often I'd wanted to go for an ice-cream with Eberhard. And now a boy I didn't **know from Adam** was inviting me for an ice-cream. Just like that. No big deal. So it can be that easy. Eberhard should **take a leaf out of his book**.

The guy was totally nice and funny and wanted to know absolutely everything about me. Then he entertained me with all sorts of crazy, funny stories, and when I told him about myself, he almost died of laughter.

I'd almost forgotten what time it was, such a pleasant time we were having in the ice-cream parlour. But then I suddenly remembered Eberhard. He was bound to be waiting already, and would be starting to get annoyed or would be wondering where I had got to.

In a total panic, I jumped up and cried: "I've got to take the dog back, sorry. It was fantastic, and thanks a million again."

Then I jogged back to our meeting point. But I could have saved myself the bother. Eberhard was,

---

ice-cream parlour – Eisdiele; to not know sb from Adam – jmdn. überhaupt nicht kennen;
to take a leaf out of sb's book – sich an jmdm. ein Beispiel nehmen

of course, not there yet. Oh great. And I had left half a dish of **ice-cream sundae**.

But then when he did come, he was really nice and sweet and apologised a thousand times over. And I was, once again, **placated** to some extent.

Friday 27th October

Lucilla was totally absolutely **over the moon** when I told her about London. She reckoned it was genuinely, **romantic in spades**.

"And totally tragic," she added. "Just now, when you've met the great love of your life, you're being torn apart." Lucilla rolled her eyes in **rapture**. "Your life is so exciting. You're so lucky, Jojo."

"That's not luck – it's *bad* luck," I corrected her.

Then she looked at me and her eyes filled with tears. "And what about us? What am I supposed to do without you?"

"Perhaps you could move house as well?" I suggested. "Quite apart from that, nothing's decided

---

ice-cream sundae – Eisbecher; to placate – versöhnen, beschwichtigen; to be over the moon – aus dem Häuschen sein; romantic in spades – total romantisch; rapture – Entzücken

yet. I don't believe we'll move. I'll simply refuse," I said decisively.

"Hey Carla, **get this**: Jojo's moving to London!" Lucilla called right across the school yard.

"Does that mean Rover, erm, sorry, Sven, will be free? I'd love to take him over, I always wanted a dog as a boyfriend. Oh, please, Jojo, have pity on me," **pleaded** Carla.

"Stupid cow," I hissed.

Lucilla put a calming arm around me. "Don't listen to her. She's just jealous."

Then I was irritated by Lucilla as well, and pretty much **at the end of my tether**.

Nobody understands me! It's the truth!

All is quiet on the London front at home. My mother is **hesitant** about turning the job down. She reckons you have to have a really good think about these things. We have to prepare ourselves mentally for moving to England, and then we can still always change our minds. 'Our' minds!

My mind is made up: not on your life!

Flippi's mind is made up too: the sooner the better.

---

get this – hör mal;
to plead – bitten und betteln;
to be at the end of one's tether – am Ende seiner Geduld sein; hesitant – zögerlich

Only my mother is **wavering**. She reckons we should try to get to like England **on a trial basis**. We should find out about the country, try to get to know its traditions and customs.

Well, if they have customs there, then the country is even more of **a no-no** for me!

But my mother was absolutely determined, and announced: "We'll begin with typical English food."

"So is there an English restaurant here?" asked Flippi, interested.

"No, **silly-billy**," laughed my mother. "I'll cook!"

On hearing that, even **hard-bitten** Flippi started to panic. "Why? We haven't done anything. Honestly. The burn mark on the living room carpet wasn't my fault!"

"Are you starting that again?" cried my mother, irritated.

This is the eternal argument in our house: my mother tries to cook although she knows full well that she can't cook. We have to suffer as **guinea pigs** and – even worse – we have to look on as she turns valuable raw material into **inedible** objects which

---

to waver – unentschlossen sein, zögern;
on a trial basis – versuchsweise; a no-no – ein Tabu;
silly-billy – Dummerchen; hard-bitten – verbissen, hartnäckig; guinea pig – Versuchskaninchen (wörtlich: Meerschweinchen); inedible – unessbar

would be sure to cause a storm of excitement at a modern art exhibition.

Every time, it causes a hideous amount of stress, and we pretty much always end up having a pizza.

"I've got to do my homework," I announced quickly, and disappeared.

Flippi wasn't far behind me. "I'll help you," she cried.

"What with?" I wanted to know.

"I can turn the pages for you," she offered **humbly**, quickly pushing me in front of her.

"No!" thundered my mother's voice. "You stay here and just explain that business about the burn mark on the living room carpet!"

"**Bummer**!" hissed Flippi. "I thought she'd not heard that one."

Our mother? Never.

Flippi hesitated. I gave her a push. "Go on, get it over with. Make sure you tell me all the details afterwards."

Then it struck me that I couldn't do my homework after all because I had to go out. To meet Eberhard, to collect the dog. I had arranged to meet Annette, and we were going to take the dogs out together. It's really brilliant that I've met her.

---

humble – demütig; bummer! – So ein Mist!

Friday evening, 27th October

When I got home that evening, I found Flippi in the kitchen, slightly **distraught**. Something traumatic must have happened to her, because she was **laying the table**.

"What's the matter with you?" I wanted to know.

"She's thinking about how to punish me," said Flippi. "But if I punish myself by **prescribing** myself a spot of kitchen duty, she might perhaps forget about it."

I didn't have a clue what Flippi was talking about.

She filled me in. Her burn mark story was, it turned out, rather more expensive than we had all thought.

The burn mark came about because of the burn-test that Flippi had to carry out. And she had to carry out the burn-test to establish what kind of material the living room carpet was made out of.

And she urgently had to know what material the carpet was made of because she had to remove a **stain**.

But my mother couldn't follow it all so quickly, and Flippi had to start again from the beginning.

"You can do a burn-test to find out what material something is made of. Wool, for example, doesn't

---

distraught – aufgewühlt; to lay the table – den Tisch decken; to prescribe – verordnen, verschreiben; stain – Fleck

burn properly – it **smoulders**. But synthetics burn and melt. So if you don't know whether something's woollen or synthetic, you do a burn-test," Flippi lectured her.

"Where on earth did you get that from?" My mother was amazed.

"From school. In the Textiles class."

"So in Textiles, you're told to go home and set fire to your carpets?" My mother was **on the verge** of having a hysterical **fit**.

"Slowly, slowly," Flippi pacified my mother, leading her to the sofa, and urging to her to sit down. Then she sat down next to my mother and held her hand. "Listen, Mummykins, just calm down first. Of course we weren't told to set fire to things. I just wanted to establish what material our carpet was made of."

"Establish what material our carpet was made of?" My mother's voice was becoming shrill again. "You turn the corner of the carpet up. It says it on the label. Under every carpet. You don't have to do a burn-test on it."

Flippi nodded bravely. "Well, yes, that would also have been a possibility. But this time I just did it differently. In any case, the carpet is pure wool. That's the good news."

---

to smoulder – schwelen; on the verge – am Rande;
fit – Anfall

"That isn't news. I knew that already!"

"Oh, good, then everything's clear," said Flippi, and decided to let the matter rest, for our mother wasn't in the best of moods right now. Flippi stood up and made as if to go to her bedroom.

"Stop, stay here. Sit back down at once," ordered our mother.

Flippi feigned surprise. "Is something else the matter?"

My mother rolled her eyes. "Don't make out you're more stupid than you are. What was all that about a stain?"

Flippi willingly sat down and beamed. "Yes, it was totally practical: the stain has gone. You see, I did the burn-test where the stain was, and the stain burned away while I was doing it. And so the whole business actually sorted itself out. Because I only wanted to know what material the carpet was made of so that I could find the right stain remover. You see, you have to use a completely different stain remover on wool from the one you use on synthetics. But **be that as it may** – the stain had gone because of the burn-test. Now that's what I call lucky!"

"That's what I call **idiocy**! And I don't even want to know what kind of stain it was!"

Flippi was offended. "Well, if that's the way you want to look at it. Can I go now?"

---

be that as it may – wie dem auch sei; idiocy – Blödsinn

Flippi has become somewhat more **subdued**.

The fact that my mother is still considering how to punish her is very much worrying Flippi.

Monday 30th October

This morning at school, Lucilla was totally offended and didn't say a word to me.

After school, I then made her explain herself: "What's wrong, Lucilla?"

Lucilla shrugged her shoulders and turned away.

I held her back. "Well, I do think you could just say why you're not talking to me."

Her bottom lip trembling, Lucilla said: "I don't know why you bother with me at all. Anyway, you've got a new friend now."

"I haven't."

"I saw you in the park together. I actually wanted to see Sven, but there wasn't a dream guy anywhere for miles. Just you two. And you've even dyed your hair the same colour so you're all coordinated. You've never done that with me. And you told me you just dyed your hair to annoy your mother."

Oh, so that was it! She was talking about Annette. Oh God, Lucilla is so **sensitive**!

---

subdued – zahm, gebändigt; sensitive – empfindlich

I laughed and put my arm round her. "Lucilla, don't be **jealous**."

"I'm not jealous," she retorted pertly.

"That's just Annette. We've only just met. The business about the hair is a total coincidence. Honestly."

"But you're bound to think she's nicer than I am."

"Rubbish. You're my best friend, as always. Honestly. You can come with us when…" I broke off because it occurred to me that we were taking the dogs out, and I'd told Lucilla that the dog belonged to our neighbour. How stupid! I always had to tell such stupid stories! Now I didn't know how to carry on.

Lucilla beamed. "Can I really come? Brilliant!"

I swallowed. I couldn't disappoint Lucilla now.

She hugged me. "You really are a brilliant friend," she cried delightedly. "See you this lunchtime, then. I have to go, I've still got a lot to do."

As she was going, she quickly turned round and asked: "What's actually going on with this Sven? Are you still together? And why don't we ever see him?"

"He's on a school trip," I called after her, amazed by how naturally these little lies slip out of me. Almost without thinking. Is that a good or a bad sign?

---

jealous – eifersüchtig

Monday evening, 30th October

When I got to the park this lunchtime Annette was already waiting for me.

We were just about to set off when someone behind us called: "Yoo-hoo! Jojo!"

I turned round and almost fainted. Lucilla was running up to us, but she looked completely changed: she had dyed her hair platinum blonde and was carrying something furry in her arms.

She beamed **excessively** happily as she reached us, stroked her hair, and said: "Well, what do you say?"

After Annette and I had said nothing – completely speechless as we were – she lifted the ball of fur into the air and said proudly: "And I've brought a dog with me, too. It belongs to one of my mother's friends. And get this: she's even paying me to take her dog out. Isn't that fantastic?"

"Unbelievable!" I cried **incredulously**.

Lucilla put the tiny ball of fur on the ground. "He's called Pooky. He's a Yorkshire Terrier. Isn't he sweet?" Then she looked at us and cried happily: "We can go!"

Annette laughed. "I think **this is a laugh**; we must look really funny, us three. What with the hair and the dogs!"

---

excessive – übermäßig; incredulous – ungläubig, skeptisch; this is a laugh – das ist echt witzig

She offered Lucilla her hand. "I'm Annette."

Then she laughed again and said to Lucilla: "Welcome to the club!"

Annette really is fantastic.

Lucilla was extremely happy and I was satisfied, too. What could go wrong? It was actually quite funny.

Lucilla bent towards me and said softly: "My mother made a terrible fuss about my new hair colour. It was a good idea of yours. It makes it clear once and for all that people of our age can't be dictated to about how we look."

I nodded absently, for I was already thinking about how I should arrange the business about handing over the dog.

Annette always leaves earlier than I do; she has different *exit times*, so to speak. So I'm normally alone when I meet up with Eberhard again. What on earth was I to do with Lucilla? Eberhard was officially on a school trip. And the dog was officially our neighbour's dog.

When Annette said goodbye, I still had no idea. I just knew one thing: I didn't want to have Lucilla with me when I met Eberhard.

"When do you actually have to get Pooky back?" I asked Lucilla **casually**.

"Doesn't matter. I can walk him for as long as I like."

---

casually – beiläufig

Now that was awkward. I thought. I still had twenty minutes before I had to take the dog back.

"What about you? When does your neighbour want her dog back? And tell me, what's he called?"

I looked at Herr Schmitt. I couldn't think of a single name. So I said: "Dog, he's just called Dog." And then I suddenly knew what to do. "And Dog has to go back home now. See you tomorrow at school, then." I turned round and dragged Herr Schmitt off with me.

All of a sudden Lucilla was by my side again. "I'll walk home with you. I've got loads of time," she cried happily.

Oh damn. **What a nuisance**. In fact I had no choice but to walk back to our house with 'Dog'.

On the way home, Lucilla suddenly tugged excitedly at my sleeve and whispered: "Don't look now, but just over there on the other side of the road, there's a guy who's staring at you the whole time. About our age, looks really fantastic. Do you know him?"

I was about to turn my head when Lucilla **hissed**: "Don't look!"

"For goodness' sake," I grumbled. "So how am I supposed to see whether I know him?"

What a nuisance! – Wie lästig/unangenehm!;
to hiss – zischen

But before Lucilla could speak, a word **resounded** across the street: “Hey!”

I looked now; of course I had to now.

Lucilla became positively agitated and quite red in the face.

“Oh my God,” she **moaned**, digging her nails firmly into my arm. “He’s coming. He’s coming over. To us!”

My arm hurt quite a lot, so I had a slightly pained expression as the guy reached us. It was the guy who had caught Herr Schmitt again.

He laughed. “Hello Jojo. Is everything okay? You look a bit down.”

“Introduce me,” whispered Lucilla in my ear, so quietly that I could **barely** hear her.

But it must very likely have been something like that, because as soon as I said to the guy: “This is my friend Lucilla,” she instantly let go of me and charmingly offered her hand to the guy.

“And this is…” Oh, how stupid. I’d completely forgotten to ask the guy his name that time.

“… my hero, the dog-catcher!” I said, and found that it **sufficed**.

He grinned at Lucilla and said: “All you have to do to impress Jojo is catch a dog.” Then he looked

---

to resound – ertönen, widerhallen;
to moan – stöhnen, jammern; barely – kaum;
to suffice – ausreichen

at me and pretended to be terribly proud. "Once I even caught **seven with one fell swoop**."

I had to laugh. He really was completely **hilarious**. I was really glad to see him.

Then he said to me: "And just in case you don't always want to address me as 'my hero', you can also call me Sven. That's what I'm actually called."

"Sven?!" Lucilla and I **shrieked** simultaneously.

Lucilla looked at me, astonished. "That's Sven?"

"No, that's not him," I said,

"Oh yes it is," said Sven the hero.

"Well, yes," I tried to appease him and to calm Lucilla down, "but that's not Sven. He's just called Sven."

Both of them looked at me as if I had **a screw loose**.

"Listen," he offered in a playfully helpful manner. "If you don't like my name, we can have a word with my parents and see if they can re-christen me. It'd be fine by me."

I had to laugh again. "No, it's fine. Actually, I think the name is positively great. But … it's just … oh, it's all too difficult to explain now."

"Then just don't try," he laughed. He really was seriously nice.

---

seven with one fell swoop – sieben auf einen Schlag;
hilarious – zum Kugeln; to shriek – kreischen;
a screw loose – eine Schraube locker

By now, Lucilla had got **infatuated** cow-eyes. Then she asked me, shocked, as quietly as she could: “So that’s not ‘your’ Sven?”

I shook my head and felt annoyed with Lucilla. I think it’s totally stupid when you whisper about people when they’re standing right next to you.

“What are you up to? Do you fancy an ice-cream?” he asked.

I shook my head.

“Chips, pizza, a trip to Rome?” he suggested further.

I had to laugh again. “I might get back to you on Rome, but now I have to get home urgently.”

“Pity,” he said, and looked as though he actually meant it.

“*I’ve* got time,” cried Lucilla. Then she gave the guy an infatuated look and murmured: “I’d love to go for an ice-cream with you if you like.”

He was a bit **put off his stroke**. He obviously wasn’t too keen on going for an ice-cream with Lucilla.

But he very probably didn’t want to say so, and so he said rather half-heartedly: “Okay.”

“Then I’m going to have an ice-cream with Sven, okay?” Lucilla said to me, and set off.

---

infatuated – vernarrt, verknallt;
to be put off one’s stroke – aus dem Rhythmus geraten

He stood where he was, undecided. So did I.

"A real pity!" he said quietly to me, then **nobly** went off with Lucilla.

I was somehow a bit disappointed, but didn't know why.

In fact, I had to go in the same direction to take Herr Schmitt back, but since I'd told Lucilla I had to go home, I couldn't very well walk along with them both now.

I was a bit confused, and then took the giant poodle home with me.

My mother was **flabbergasted** when I appeared at the living room door with a King Poodle.

"That's going too far, Jojo. That dog is not coming in my house," she declared, placing herself defensively in the doorway.

"Just for five minutes! Please!" I begged.

"No," said my mother and closed the door.

So I sat on the doorstep in front of the door with Herr Schmitt, and waited for the time to pass.

When I was sure that Lucilla was out of sight, I crept back along the road with Herr Schmitt and raced back with record-breaking speed to meet Eberhard.

We both arrived with our tongues hanging out.

---

noble – edel, großmütig;
to be flabbergasted – völlig platt sein

Eberhard was waiting, already somewhat impatiently.

"Are you training the dog for the Olympics?" he asked.

"It's part of his education and upbringing," I replied in an expert-sounding tone. I don't let anyone **interfere** when I'm doing dog-training.

"Oh, and what are you teaching him?"

"Running," I said, and when it struck me that this was rather a weak explanation, I added: "The dog just has to learn that his master dictates the speed and he has to adapt to it."

That sounded good; Eberhard seemed impressed. "You know what you're doing," he said. "But it's a real pity you're so late; I wanted to go and have an ice-cream with you both. But I've got to go now, or Herr Schmitt will get home too late. See you tomorrow, then, little angel. And thanks a million for dog-sitting as well."

With that he was gone, and I stood there kicking myself until I was blue in the face.

Oh brilliant. Today of all days he had time for me, and I was too late.

And all that just because of platinum blonde Lucilla and Pooky. **For goodness' sake**: Pooky – what kind of name is that? Dog owners really are **nuts**.

---

to interfere – sich einmischen; For goodness' sake! – Um Gottes willen!; to be nuts – verrückt sein

Then I ran after Eberhard and called: “Wait a minute!”

He turned round, somewhat alarmed. “What is it?” he asked.

I actually wanted to suggest to him that we could go for an ice-cream together tomorrow, but since he seemed so unfriendly all of a sudden, I no longer dared.

“I’m really sorry I was late,” I said instead.

“Don’t worry about it,” he said graciously.

“If … if it’s so important to you to go for an ice-cream with me, we could do it tomorrow,” I stammered.

He thought for a moment.

Stupidly enough, I then added ‘please’, which of course **put paid to** my coolness. Oh, I never learn!

He smiled. “**All sorted**, little angel. Tomorrow afternoon we’ll go for an ice-cream together.”

I beamed.

“But I really do have to go now!” he said and trotted off. Then he turned round once again and called: “Start thinking about what sort of ice-cream you want.”

I nodded. Anything, just not raspberry. I’m allergic to it.

---

to put paid to – zunichte machen, zerstören;
all sorted – alles klar

Then I grew **bolder**. "We could go to the cinema too," I called after him.

He stopped, turned round, and said: "Okay. Ice-cream first, then cinema. Fine!"

I felt a shock of delight. It had been so easy!

First ice-cream, then cinema. It will be the best day of my life!

Life is simply wonderful. How could anyone be this lucky?

Now I just have to find some way to get rid of Lucilla tomorrow.

Tuesday 31th October

Ha! Life loves me. My Lucilla-problem has been solved: Lucilla rang after school to say that she was afraid she couldn't come today because it was her grandmother's birthday and she had to go out with her mother.

I was over the moon. Only internally, of course. That was generous of me indeed.

But then, unfortunately, everything became complicated after all.

Because Lucilla said: "Could you do me a favour, please?"

---

bold – kühn, gewagt

"Anything!" I said cheerfully, because Lucilla had just solved a problem for me. I could have hugged her. But then I didn't know that she was going to create another problem for me half a minute later.

"It's about Pooky," she said. "I had promised to take him for a walk again today. And I thought you might perhaps be able to take him with you. You're going anyway."

I didn't say anything, because I had to think how I could get out of it.

"You can keep the money, too."

"Money?" I asked.

"Yes, I told you: I get paid for taking Pooky out. Perhaps you should have a word with your neighbour sometime. Perhaps she'd pay you too for taking Dog out." What neighbour? And who's Dog? What was Lucilla on about? Oh, yeah, right. I was the one who had come out with all that nonsense.

"Erm, listen, I just do it for the love of **humanity**. But if Pooky's old dear wants to give me the money, that's fine."

"You're a **gem**, Josie. Say hello to Annette from me. See you!"

"Stop, wait a minute," I called quickly. I still had a question, but didn't know exactly how to formulate it.

---

humanity – die Menschheit;
gem – Juwel, Schatz

"Hey, Lucilla, so how was it yesterday? At the ice-cream parlour? With the guy?"

Lucilla giggled.

I became annoyed. "Oh, just spit it out," I demanded.

"Oh," **piped** Lucilla, "he's totally sweet. He wanted to know thousands of things about me."

"Seriously?" Somehow a feeling of jealousy spread over me. No idea why. "What, then?"

"Oh, things about you, what you do and stuff."

I was hugely pleased, but just said: "Oh, right, well, then."

"Tell me, Jojo, do you like him?"

"Naah!"

"So can I have him? You see, I think he's totally sweet."

Again, a hot feeling of jealousy shot up within me. But I just said: "Sounds okay. Have fun at your grandmother's."

"Yeah, right. But thanks all the same."

I was a bit confused because I was aware of how much the idea of Lucilla **befriending** Sven irritated me. But then I thought to myself: I'm just being really stupid. I've got Eberhard, I'm totally **besotted** with him, so Lucilla can go out with Sven as much as she likes. I don't mind.

---

to pipe – flöten; to befriend sb – sich mit jmdm. anfreunden; to be besotted with – verknallt sein in

And, what's more, I was even going to go to the cinema today. With Eberhard, the absolute dream guy. How about that?

And Lucilla's out of the way, and little Pooky is no big deal. Plus, I'll even get money for it… I'd do that any day.

I decided that today was simply my lucky day.

Tuesday evening, 31th October

It was a very average lucky day.

First I collected Pooky. He really is more like a little handbag-sized rat. Tiny. But really sweet. And then I went to the park.

I couldn't help **skipping** the whole time because I was so totally happy and was just so looking forward to the ice-cream and the cinema.

Eberhard was a bit annoyed when he saw Pooky. "Are you taking strange dogs out?" he asked suspiciously.

"Of course not," I immediately put his mind at rest.

"So who does that dog belong to?" he wanted to know.

In fact I thought that it was none of his business,

---

to skip – hüpfen, springen

but I could hardly say so. After all, I wanted to go for an ice-cream and to the cinema with him, so I didn't want to ruin the good atmosphere.

I smiled. "Well, who do you think he belongs to?" That's a totally cool trick: when you don't know the answer to a question, reply with a counter-question.

Eberhard frowned, then he laughed. "It's *your* dog. So why didn't you say anything?"

Well, why *didn't* I say anything? My dog? Not a bad idea.

Eberhard **tickled** Pooky behind the ears.

"He's quite sweet. A bit un-dog-like, but okay," he said.

I felt so content. It was as if Eberhard were tickling *me* behind the ears. And that's almost what he was doing, as I had Pooky under my arm.

"So, I've got to go now. We'll see each other later. Then we'll go for an ice-cream," he said.

"And to the cinema," I reminded him.

"Oh, yes, erm… there's a problem with that."

Oh no, please not. No problem!

"The thing is… we'll have to **postpone** it."

"Oh?" was all I could say, and I tried pretty hard to make sure he couldn't see my disappointment. That very first time I took his strange dog out, he offered to take me for an ice-cream and to the cine-

---

to tickle – kitzeln;
to postpone – verschieben

ma sometime. And now I've already spent the longest time of my entire life running around the place with the dog, and nothing's happening. It's really **mean**.

"But we'll make up for it. Honestly. I'm quite desperate to go to the cinema with you," he **assured** me.

Quite desperate?

"Why?" I asked, offended.

He smiled a quite lovely smile. "Because I think you're totally sweet."

Oh, sigh! He's so-o-o sweet. And so lovely.

"So why can't we go to the cinema today?" I asked, already almost placated again.

"I have **to step in for** a friend. He reads stories to the residents at the old people's home every evening."

Wow, I was really impressed. It really does seem to be totally in, this good-deed stuff.

"You understand, don't you, little angel?"

I nodded and **swallowed**.

"I'd far rather go to the cinema with you," he murmured **abjectly**. "You do believe me, don't you?"

Too right I do!

---

mean – gemein; to assure – ermutigen, versichern;
Oh, sigh! – Ach! Seufz!;
to step in for sb – für jmdn. einspringen;
to swallow – schlucken; abject – unterwürfig

"It's okay," I said, because I was afraid that he might start **whining** and begging for **mercy**, and I don't like that sort of thing.

"You're a treasure," he said and gave me quite a fond hug.

Now I wasn't just completely placated, but was **on cloud nine** again too. Well, then, if he's not mad about me, then I don't know what. All the classic signs point to it.

In that case, you can easily postpone an odd evening at the cinema.

"When are we going to the cinema?"

He thought. "Next week?"

"When?" I wasn't about to give up so quickly.

"Wednesday?"

"Monday!" I demanded.

"Okay, Tuesday," he gave in.

"Okay, Tuesday." I accepted the compromise.

Then he rushed off and I walked round the park with Herr Schmitt and Pooky.

In the park, people constantly kept making stupid remarks about the two dogs, because Pooky is so tiny and Herr Schmitt so **inordinately** large. I found it just too stupid, so I finally took Pooky under my arm so that nobody could see him any more. The poor chap got nothing of his walk; he didn't even

---

to whine – winseln; mercy – Gnade;
on cloud nine – auf Wolke sieben; inordinate – unmäßig

get to run. But at least he was out in the fresh air. Perhaps I'll just let her give me half the money.

I was almost back to my normal good mood when I then met Eberhard and we set off for the ice-cream parlour. I wanted to go inside, but he stayed outside and asked for two ice-creams.

"What kind d'you want?" he called to me.

I was a bit irritated. "Why aren't we going in?" I asked.

Eberhard looked rather anxiously into the ice-cream parlour and said: "Oh, let's just go for a bit of a walk."

I opened my eyes wide. Go for a walk? I'd just spent two hours walking through the park! Why on earth should I go for a walk now? I wanted to sit down and dine in style on an ice-cream. Should I insist? I started to feel really cross.

Eberhard put his head on one side, looked at me with faithful puppy eyes, and begged: "Please. For my sake."

I rolled my eyes. "Fine."

It's difficult to be angry with him. He's just got a way about him…

So we both walked through the park again with an ice-cream in one hand and a dog lead in the other. I knew **the ins and outs** of every tree; I was already **on first-name terms** with them.

---

the ins and outs – jedes Detail; on first-name terms – per du

Somehow, I was disappointed and angry with him. But I also felt a bit stupid for feeling like this, because he really hadn't done anything that bad. It was more what he *didn't* do that annoyed me.

Someone else might be able to make something of my feelings. But not me at any rate. Whatever, my mood was **up the spout**. But I didn't let him see it.

After the ice-cream I took Pooky back and then, in a bad mood, trotted home.

On the way home I met Sven.

"Hello," he cried cheerfully. Then he looked at me in **mock** fear. "Your friend isn't lurking anywhere by any chance, is she?"

I laughed. "Nah, don't worry, **the coast's clear**."

"Just don't do anything like that to me again," he said.

"Like what?" I asked, surprised.

"Well, sending along a **substitute** woman when I want to go for an ice-cream with you."

"Hey, listen, I never…"

"It's okay," he interrupted, and laughed. "It was my own fault."

"Precisely," I said.

---

to be up the spout – im Eimer sein; mock – Schein, scheinbar; the coast's clear – die Luft ist rein; substitute – Ersatz

I was somehow still in a bad mood because of Eberhard, and he most probably noticed it.

"What's the matter? Problems with your mother?"

"Nah."

"Your sister?"

"Nah."

"Your teacher?"

"Nah." My mood was already starting to improve.

He hesitated slightly. "Your boyfriend?"

Aha, so that was the **crucial** question.

"Nah."

"What do you mean, nah? No problem, or no boyfriend?"

I had to grin. The guy really was kind of sweet.

"No boyfriend," I said, and felt bad. Why didn't I say anything about Eberhard?

"Is that the reason why you're in a bad mood?"

"What reason?"

"Because you haven't got a boyfriend."

I laughed.

"Because if that's a problem, I could help you out," he offered.

I caught my breath. Was that a **proposal**?

"What have you got in mind?" I asked cautiously.

He grinned. "I could stick an **advert** in the newspaper for you: sweet blonde seeks boyfriend. Con-

---

crucial – entscheidend; proposal – Angebot, Antrag; advert – Anzeige dition: he can't be called Sven. She has a problem with that name."

I did laugh, but I was also a bit disappointed. I'd somehow hoped for a different answer. I suddenly thought: it's possible that he just wants to make fun of me. Well, that's just what I needed. My mood didn't improve in the slightest.

On the contrary, it quite suddenly became even worse and I just said shortly: "I've got to go home. Bye." I turned and just left him standing there.

He was so gobsmacked that he neither said a word nor ran after me.

Fine, see if I care.

And now I was in a doubly bad mood.

Oh great.

Wednesday 1st November

My bad mood persisted as I made my way to the park with Herr Schmitt this afternoon.

I was even really cross with Eberhard. It's pretty weird, I thought, that the guy never has time for me. And then I felt cross with myself, because it's always the same: when he's there in front of me, beaming at me, being so grateful and calling me angel, I just can't be cross with him any more. Nobody could.

But now, when he was miles away, I was cross.

When I met Annette, I complained about Eberhard.

And she, in fact, thought I was right, too. "Exactly, Jojo, you put up with too much from that guy. He really doesn't have much time for you. But you can take his stupid dog out. **You'll do for that**."

That was too much. I was really angry. "Herr Schmitt isn't stupid. Your Mops is stupid… and some. Herr Schmitt doesn't slobber, and if he runs off, you can at least call his name out loud!"

"What are you on about, Jojo? I'm talking about Sven and the way he treats you!"

I was totally **astounded**. "Sven? What? How does he treat me?"

What did she know about Sven? Then it struck me that she actually meant Eberhard. I really have created a **muddle** with these names. But who could guess that I'd meet a guy called Sven?

"He's totally sweet and lovely," I defended Eberhard.

"But you said yourself that he's hardly got any time for you!"

"It's not his fault if he has so little time."

"You're totally blind!"

"Love does make you blind!" I cried, annoyed, and

---

you'll do for that – dafür bist du gut genug;
astounded – erstaunt;
muddle – Durcheinander, Kuddelmuddel

then didn't exactly know myself why I had said that. Annette rolled her eyes, irritated.

I was angry. "Well, it's your turn to say something now! What's going on with your Edgar? How many times have you been to the cinema together? He never has time either!"

"That's different. He has to study for school. And anyway, we went to the cinema together yesterday."

"If he's such a **swot** that he studies day and night, there's no way he can be as good looking as you always say he is. You can say all you like, but I've never seen him."

"So? I've never laid eyes on your Sven either. Edgar looks fantastic! What's more, there's no connection between being good at school and what you look like. Is there?"

She was right somewhere along the line, but I just said: "Well, all right."

We walked in silence for a while.

Annette gave me a **sidelong look**. "You know what, Jojo? We shouldn't quarrel about boys. Women shouldn't ever quarrel about men. They're not worth it."

I didn't know exactly what she meant, but I didn't in fact want to quarrel with Annette either. It was always good fun with her. The stupid dog-walking was no longer as boring because of her.

---

swot – Streber; a sidelong look – ein Seitenblick

I nodded.

"Perhaps you ought to give him an ultimatum. Something along the lines of 'go out with me, or **I'm off**'," suggested Annette.

"Don't start again!" I grumbled.

Annette laid a pacifying arm round my shoulders. "Listen, Jojo, strictly speaking you're right. I reckon that Edgar has too little time for me, too. He's **not a jot** better than your Sven. We were actually going to go for an ice-cream yesterday and then on to the cinema. But then he appeared and said we couldn't do the ice-cream, but we could go to the cinema. He said he wouldn't have time until the evening."

That **appeased** me somewhat.

"There you go – and I went for an ice-cream but not to the cinema. It's the same."

"Cinema is in a different league from going for an ice-cream," Annette informed me. "And I don't mean that in a horrible way," she quickly added.

I nodded. "You're right. I'll insist that he takes me to the cinema. At the end of the day, he did promise."

Annette nodded. "And I shall insist on my ice-cream."

We were then both in a much better mood and

I'm off – ich haue ab; not a jot – kein bisschen;
to appease – versöhnen

talked about something else. Annette is really brilliant.

When Lucilla appeared, I asked Annette not to talk about Sven in front of her, and Annette didn't even ask why not. I think that sort of thing is fantastic.

Shortly afterwards, Annette had to go, and Lucilla wanted to go home earlier, thank God, so I could hand Herr Schmitt over without any problems.

I reminded Eberhard once again about our Tuesday cinema date and he said: "I can hardly wait."

"We can always go earlier if you don't want to wait so long," I offered.

But he just laughed and said: "You're really sweet!"

Then he went.

And 'really sweet' Jojo stood there. Alone. Not in a particularly good mood.

Why on earth not?

Friday 3rd November

There was a bit of stress with Eberhard yesterday. I had to go to the dentist's. Nothing special, just a routine thing. My mother insists that we present our teeth to the dentist at regular intervals. Fine, if that's what she wants.

I thought that it would just fit in time-wise if Eberhard collected Herr Schmitt on time. Because he is sometimes late, I asked him to be punctual this time.

"No problem, little angel. You can rely on me."

Right! Not a bit of it. Who didn't arrive on time? Mr 'No Problem'. I was really cross. And in real trouble.

What was I supposed to do with Herr Schmitt?

I decided to take him to the dentist's. But they wouldn't let me in with the dog **in tow**. For 'reasons of hygiene'. I was really annoyed and ran back to the park where I waited again for Eberhard. Nothing.

So I went back to the dentist's. Tried again. No luck. Even though I had the **presence of mind** to suggest that the dentist could check Herr Schmitt's teeth as well. He wasn't interested, he said.

I think he might have been kind of cross, because his name is, unfortunately, Herr Schmitt as well – or rather Dr Schmitt. And when I kept going on about Herr Schmitt and pointing to the dog, he most probably thought I was trying to **take the mickey**, and so became rather unfriendly.

So I rang Flippi and asked her to come over and take Herr Schmitt. The dog, not the dentist.

Flippi demanded two euros for doing it. Okay, I was desperate, so I paid up.

---

in tow – im Schlepptau; presence of mind – Geistesgegenwart; to take the mickey – jmdn. veralbern

"And how am I supposed to recognise the guy for the **handover**? Have you got a password?"

"What? Why would I need one of those?"

"Well, I don't want to give the dog to **any odd person**. Haven't you ever heard of dog-napping?"

"Dog what?"

"Dog-napping! Kidnapping – dog-napping."

"Oh, Flippi, what's all this rubbish about? Nobody would take this dog home with them of their own free will. I can guarantee you that nobody but Eber... erm, Sven, will want this dog."

Then something else occurred to me. "Oh, by the way, don't call him Sven. He doesn't like it much. Don't address him by any name at all. Okay?"

Flippi shook her head. "You do have some strange friends."

I became a bit unsure. "You'll get another euro if you promise."

Flippi sensed a chance. "Add another euro to it, and I'll not say a single word to him. I'll act as if I were **dumb**," she offered.

I thought quickly, but decided that it was a complete swindle, demanding money for saying nothing.

"Get a move on, and don't ruin things!" I ordered, and disappeared into the dentist's surgery.

---

handover – Übergabe; any odd person – irgendeiner, ein X-Beliebiger; dumb – stumm

Of course, then there were complications after all. Well, only a small, rather embarrassing one.

Flippi said, you see: “Jojo’s at the dentist.”

And that **nitwit** Eberhard actually asked: “Who’s Jojo?”

And Flippi, the idiot, answered: “She’s the stupid platinum-blonde cow who you **fob** this mutt **off on** while you’re out having fun, God knows where!”

Flippi said ‘Sven’ had become a bit annoyed, had taken the dog, and had **sloped off**.

I was torn two ways. On the one hand, I think it’s good that Flippi was cheeky to him, and on the other hand, I hope he’s not annoyed with me now.

Especially because we’re going to the cinema on Tuesday. If Flippi has messed that up, she’s in for it. Lucilla asked me about Sven this morning at school.

“Why should I know where he’s got to? It doesn’t make the slightest bit of difference to me either,” I snapped at her.

“Sorry for being born. Wow, you really are in a bad mood,” Lucilla said crossly.

“I’m sorry Lucilla,” I said at once. “I’ve somehow … oh, I don’t know. Everything is so complicated.”

“With Sven?”

I looked at her, astonished.

---

nitwit – Schwachkopf;
to fob sth off on sb – jmdm. etwas aufhalsen;
to slope off – sich trollen

"Oh, you mean with *my* Sven. I thought you were talking about..."

"Yes, I mean *your* Sven. Not *mine*," explained Lucilla.

It annoyed me that Lucilla just talked about 'her' Sven. There's no way it could have got to that stage yet.

And I was annoyed with myself again for just calling Eberhard 'Sven' and for constantly getting myself mixed up. You need to know where you are! But I really can't **undo** it now.

"No-o-o, everything's okay." I didn't want to admit that things weren't going so well.

"I absolutely have to see your Sven sometime, Jojo."

And *I* have to see *yours*, I thought, then asked myself: why, actually? But all I said to Lucilla was: "It's bound to happen at some point."

Saturday 4th November

And it happened today.

Eberhard didn't create any stress about yesterday. He's a very forgiving guy. He even apologised to me for being late yesterday. How about that?

---

to undo sth – etw. ungeschehen machen

"Did you get into **strife** because of it?" he wanted to know.

"Me? Nah. It wasn't a problem at all."

"Thank God," he said, relieved. "I was afraid that you might be annoyed and that you'd cancel our cinema date."

"**Not on your life!**" it slipped out of me. Which was immediately rather embarrassing because it didn't exactly sound very cool. But it was too late.

He grinned. "Well, everything's fine then."

"Yoo-hoo!" a voice came from behind me.

I turned round, and it was Lucilla. She was waving at me like a windmill.

"I have to go," I said quickly to Eberhard.

Thank God I already had Herr Schmitt's lead in my hand. I ran to Lucilla, who didn't notice me in the slightest, but stared at Eberhard.

"Is that him?" she asked incredulously.

I also looked at him. Yes, he did look fantastic. I waved to him once again and dragged Lucilla off in the opposite direction.

"Yes," I said quite casually.

"Wow, he's good looking," sighed Lucilla and sank down against a lamp post. "Jojo, you lucky cow!"

I enjoyed Lucilla's admiration.

"How long's he been back?" asked Lucilla.

"Back?" I didn't know what Lucilla was talking about.

---

strife – Ärger, Streit; Not on your life! – Auf keinen Fall!

"From the school trip!"

I pondered about what Lucilla might possibly mean. Had seeing Eberhard **cast** her into such a confused state that she was now talking in a fever?

But then it struck me again. I am a stupid cow. If you've got a bad memory, you shouldn't tell stories. It's bound to go wrong sooner or later.

"Since today," I said quickly.

Lucilla looked even more dreamy. "And he has to see you at once. How romantic!" Then a shocked expression came over her face. "Did I disturb you in some way? I mean, you'd surely prefer to go for a walk with Sven, wouldn't you?"

"With Sven?" I asked, **caught out**, and looked at her wide-eyed. Oh, right, I then realised, Lucilla means Eberhard of course. I smiled at Lucilla graciously. "No, that's fine, I told him that I wanted to spend a bit of time with my best friend. He understands that."

"Wow, Jojo, that's really brilliant of you."

I suddenly felt bad. Really terrible. I shouldn't do things like that. Yes, Lucilla can be annoying sometimes, but she's basically really nice. Why can't I just tell her the truth?

Well, because the truth doesn't actually sound so good. Depressing, rather. I dye my hair a colour I

---

to cast – werfen; caught out – ertappt

don't particularly like. I walk all over the place with a dog although dogs aren't my thing. And all to please a good-looking guy. It's kind of sad, isn't it? And I'm jealous that my friend likes a guy who I don't actually want anything to do with. Yes, Sven's totally nice, but I'm mad about Eberhard. But somehow things aren't going as planned with this Eberhard. I just don't know where I am.

Okay, this is how we'll do it: I'll go to the cinema with him. And either something clear happens so that I can be quite certain that he thinks I'm totally brilliant and is serious about us, or that's it. Curtains. *Finito.* Then he can take his dog out on his own.

Suddenly Lucilla dug her nails into my arm and squeaked: "Oh my God, there he is!"

"Who?"

"Him!"

Sven came over to us. I was really glad to see him.

"I think I'd better walk a bit of the way with you. For safety reasons," he said.

"For safety reasons?" I asked, irritated. "Are you concerned about my safety?" I said **coquettishly**, suddenly feeling in a good mood.

"Don't be ridiculous, of course I'm not worried about yours. About Herr Schmitt's. In case he's attacked by a rabbit or something."

---

coquettish – frech, kokett

I had to laugh. It really was crazy, the way I could always laugh so easily with Sven.

"My dog ran away last week too," Lucilla piped up.

"Which dog?" asked Sven, looking around on the floor. He made out that he couldn't see Pooky.

Lucilla was slightly offended.

Sven saw it, and immediately said in a conciliatory way: "The dog is really sweet. He goes well with you."

And Lucilla beamed and went red.

Unfortunately, I became rather jealous.

"Are you doing anything today?" he asked Lucilla.

I was completely **stunned**, and seriously hurt.

Lucilla pulled a totally remorseful face. "I'm afraid so. We've got visitors, and I've got to go home in a minute."

Sven nodded, turned to me and grinned. "Then it looks as if I'll have **to make do with** you. How about a pizza?"

"How about Rome?" I asked **high-spiritedly**.

"Now, just don't rush things. Always take things one step at a time. First pizza, and if I see that you know how to eat with a knife and fork, then it's Rome's turn."

---

to be stunned – wie betäubt sein; to make do with sb – sich zufrieden geben mit jmdm; high-spirited – übermütig

"I only eat pizza with my hands."

Sven frowned and said regretfully: "Then it'll have to be Florence at best."

I had to laugh again.

"And what about Sven?" Lucilla suddenly asked.

I got a shock of the first order. The blood shot into my head.

Sven put his head on one side. "Precisely: what about Sven?" he asked very sweetly.

"No, I mean Jojo's boyfriend."

Sven looked at Lucilla, astonished.

"He's called Sven, too," babbled Lucilla cheerfully. "Isn't that a strange coincidence?"

Now Sven looked me straight in the eye. "Is that true?" he asked me.

I turned, looked remorseful, and couldn't **utter** a single word.

He nodded. "Thanks. That was a revealing answer." Then he turned ironic: "You really didn't have to say so much."

He looked around the park. "Oh, I can see a dog in trouble over there. I think I'd better step in. After all, I'm the rescuer of dogs and blondes." And with that he disappeared.

Lucilla laughed. "He's really funny, don't you think Jojo?"

I had to swallow; I had a **lump** in my throat. Then

---

to utter – äußern; lump – (hier:) Kloß

I said to myself: **I don't give a toss** what Sven thinks of me. I'm going to the cinema with Eberhard and that's going to be my big day.

What do I care about Sven?!

Tuesday 7th November

It's make-or-break today. One wrong word and we're finished. Honestly.

I've had a think, you see: Eberhard finally has to show some commitment now. I mean, seriously for once. What has he done for me so far? He brought me a nougat ring. We've had an ice-cream once. Holding them in our hands while walking along. How romantic, hahaha. And we went for a walk together with Herr Schmitt once. Right at the start.

Since then, we've honestly only seen each other at the dog-handover. That really is pretty pathetic.

If the cinema business goes well today, I'll carry on. Otherwise, that's it. I'm not stupid.

Oh, sigh! But I am in love. And how. He's just so fantastically sweet. And he's actually really lovely to me. I have to try to understand his situation. I'm sure he'd love to spend more time with me, too.

Perhaps I shouldn't be so hard. He does at least

I don't give a toss – es ist mir völlig egal

call me little angel. And he wouldn't do that if he didn't like me. And he said twice that I was sweet. And he brought me a nougat ring. And he took a bite of my nougat ring.

I think there are in fact a lot of things pointing to him being in love with me.

Apart from that, I'm so much in love with him that it's enough for both of us. Oh, I can hardly wait to go to the cinema with him. It's sure to be totally brilliant!

Wednesday 8th November

Okay, that's it.

It's finished. Once and for all. I hate him! And it's good that way. I'm already feeling much better.

I cried for hours yesterday evening and was in complete **despair**. But this morning I **made a resolution** not to waste any more tears on Eberhard. He's **not remotely** earned it. And why should he, either! Huh! Just because he looks so sweet and is so charming and…

Boo-hoo, it's so awful. Now I have to cry yet again.

---

despair – Verzweiflung;
to make a resolution – einen Entschluss fassen;
not remotely – nicht im Entferntesten

It's so unfair! He's so sweet! I hate him. He's so-o-o mean!

Not another word about Eberhard. The topic is closed. Every tiny piece of paper I write his name on is wasted!

How on earth could he do it? He *promised!* What's more – just look at me. I'd told everyone that I was going to the cinema with him!

And then the stupid idiot arrived, put on his faithful puppy dog look, and said: "Little angel, I've got a problem."

It didn't remotely occur to me that it could have anything to do with our evening cinema date, and I said cheerfully: "Oh, problems are there to be solved. What's it all about?"

He beamed. "I really am so glad that you're so **chilled out** about it. You really have got **a fantastic take on** life."

I was riding a wave with all this praise. "That's just the way I am."

He hugged me and said: "You're a real angel."

I felt quite faint with joy and I beamed even more madly.

He was quite happy. "You really do make it easy for me. Anyone else would have **kicked up a real stink**."

---

to be chilled out (slang) – völlig 'cool' sein;
a fantastic take on sth (slang) – eine tolle Auffassung von etw.;
to kick up a real stink – richtig stinksauer werden

"Well, *I'm* not like the others," I cried, still cheerful and unsuspecting, and hoped that he'd give me another hug any minute if I stayed this nice and chilled out.

"But," he said ingenuously, "there's always another time."

I nodded. And stopped short. What was he talking about?

I became mildly suspicious and asked: "What's this all about, then?"

He looked at me wide-eyed. "Haven't I mentioned it yet?"

"I certainly didn't catch it anyway. So, at the risk of repeating yourself, just say **outright** what your problem is," I suggested, becoming somewhat more suspicious.

I had the feeling that I was in for something that I wasn't going to like in the slightest.

And the next minute it happened.

"The cinema," he said. "I'm afraid I can't make it tonight."

I stared at him.

"But I'm really glad you're so chilled out about it all," he **avowed** and beamed at me.

But I wasn't in the slightest bit chilled out about it. Quite the reverse. I was a mixture of completely

---

outright – gerade heraus;
to avow – offen bekennen, gestehen

devastated and so angry I could spit fire. But I couldn't respond at all.

"You know, the thing is, this evening I've got to…" he began.

"It's fine," I interrupted him immediately. I didn't want to hear yet another stupid explanation.

I pressed Herr Schmitt's lead into his hand and said: "I'm afraid I haven't got time to go to the cinema with you today. I hope you're not cross."

Then I turned and went. Tears were already running down my face.

"Hey, little angel, wait a minute…" he called after me, but I increased my pace and **fled**. All I needed now was for him to see me bawling.

So that was a **dignified** exit. He didn't cancel me: I cancelled him. Serves him right. I won't stand for that. I really did do right there.

Now I just wonder why I feel so miserable and why I spent the whole night crying.

I hate him. Honestly. That's it. Not another single word about that guy!

---

to flee – fliehen;
dignified – würdevoll

Thursday 9th November

I shan't waste a single line more on Eberhard! That's it. At the end of the day, there are enough important and exciting things in my life. Ha!

But now I just have to cry every time I see any stupid dog. Must be missing Herr Schmitt.

When Lucilla asked me at school about Sven (and I realised in time that she meant Eberhard), tears **welled up** in my eyes.

She was quite shocked, but I managed to calm her down and convince her that I'd got something in my eye. And then I asked her not to talk about Sven any more. Of course, she wanted to know why.

I told her I'd promised my mother that I'd not mention boys for a week but would just concentrate on school.

"Your mother is really strange… *really* strange," said Lucilla, and I said: "You can say that again," and Lucilla said: "I did!", and then, thank God, I had to laugh, and the subject was closed.

Lucilla rang me in the afternoon. "Guess who I met!"

"No idea."

"Sven!"

A shiver ran through me. "Oh? And?"

---

to well up – hervorquellen

"He really is totally sweet."

"Hmm. Which Sven?"

"My Sven! I'm not supposed to be talking about yours, am I?"

"Oh, yes. And?"

"I asked him if he'd go to the cinema with me."

I was cross.

"But he didn't have time."

I was quite relieved.

"You know what I reckon, Jojo?"

"No-o, what?"

"I reckon something's wrong with him. He seems kind of depressed. And he's normally in a really good mood."

I was aware that I'd suddenly **pricked up my ears** and was seized by a slight **thrill**. "So what do you think's the matter with him?" I asked Lucilla. "Has he said anything?"

"No he hasn't. But I'll take care of him. Maybe he needs someone to talk to."

And **thump!** My mood **slumped** back down into the basement. Somehow I didn't want Lucilla to take care of him.

But then it occurred to me again that it had nothing at all to do with me. **That wasn't my business**.

---

to prick up one's ears – hellhörig werden; thrill – Schauer; thump! – plumps!; to slump – sacken;
That wasn't my business! – Das ging mich nichts an!

I, after all, had Eberhard – who I was totally furious with; was crying my eyes out for; and who I never wanted to see again. And that was more than enough to keep me busy.

Friday 10th November

I'm not **dedicating** a single line more to him. Oh, **snivel** and double snivel. I'm so unhappy! My life is awful. I miss him. Herr Schmitt, of course. Not Eberhard. I couldn't care less about him.

Perhaps I'll just go for a bit of a walk in the park. I need some exercise. And going out in the fresh air is healthy, too.

I just hope I don't happen to meet Eberhard. It really would annoy me if I were to bump into him. I could of course go for a walk somewhere else, where there's less of a risk of **encountering** him, but I refuse to stay away from the park **on the off chance** that Eberhard might be there!

Pah, I couldn't care less about that **so-and-so**. He doesn't interest me one tiny bit.

---

to dedicate – widmen; to snivel – schnüffeln, wimmern; to encounter – begegnen; on the off chance – für den unwahrscheinlichen Fall; a so-and-so – ein Mistkerl

I'll just quickly put on a bit of make-up, and change into something cool. And I just hope that I don't bump into Eberhard.

Friday evening, 10th November

Oh, Eberhard is so-o-o sweet. Honestly. It was all just a misunderstanding. I really was a bit unfair. Oh well, we all make mistakes sometimes. He wasn't in the slightest bit cross with me, either.

It was honestly pure chance that I met him. He was walking Herr Schmitt through the park, rather bad-temperedly it seemed to me.

I wondered whether I should say hello to him, then I thought it would be better if he spoke to me first.

And that's in fact what he did the very minute he spotted me. "Hey," he called. "Long time no see!"

Since he was acting as if nothing were wrong, I followed suit.

"Hi Sv…," I almost said Sven. I'd got so used to the name that I could only just stop myself. So I just repeated, "Hi".

"So where have you been all this time?" he asked cheerfully.

"Oh, I've had a lot to do," was all I said. He doesn't absolutely have to know that I'm annoyed with him.

"Do you want to walk with me a bit?" he suggested.

I shrugged my shoulders. "I could do," I said graciously.

"Brilliant." He seemed genuinely pleased.

It's possible that I did over-react a bit really. Oh well. We all do it sometimes.

We walked through the park for a bit. I didn't say much because I didn't know what to say.

"Do you want an ice-cream?" he asked.

"Okay," I said, and resolved not to be annoyed if it was just a takeaway ice-cream again.

"But I'll pay for my own ice-cream," I **clarified**. I wanted to prove to him that I was totally independent and absolutely did not need him to pay for my ice-cream.

"Oh, come on, you'll surely let me buy you an ice-cream," he said in a most gentlemanly manner. "After all, you've taken Herr Schmitt out for me **loads of** times."

Ha, he hasn't forgotten, and nor does he **take it for granted**. How wrong my mother was about him!

He bought me an ice-cream and we went for a walk. Somehow it was totally great. We chatted and he was so-o-o lovely to me again. I really started to **long for** him and was already regretting having

---

to clarify – klären; loads of – viel; to take sth for granted – etw. als selbstverständlich hinnehmen;
to long for sb – sich nach jmdm. sehnen

gone to ground for a couple of days. And then only one thing mattered to me: for him to ask me to take Herr Schmitt out for him again.

And he asked me to do it, too. But it was even better than that. He said: "Know what? It's much more fun taking Herr Schmitt out with you. Are you free any time tomorrow? If so, we could meet and walk through the park together."

I was happier than happy. "Of course," I said immediately. Then I remembered something. "What about the homework, then?"

"Oh, I always get that out of the way straight off."

"No-o, I mean at the children's home."

"Oh, that homework! Er…yes, a friend's doing it for me now."

Oh, fantastic. We had time for one another at last! Now things really could start to happen. I was in seventh heaven. Eberhard was in a really great mood, and was genuinely mega-nice to me. I'd almost made the most gigantic mistake with that one.

I **floated** happily home and could hardly wait to see him again the next day.

I even felt bad because I'd been unfair to him.

He's so-o-o-o-o-o sweet.

On the way home I met Sven.

---

to go to ground – sich verstecken; to float – schweben

I was in such a good mood that I ran up to him.

“Hey, how are you? Haven’t seen you **for ages**,” I cried cheerfully.

He was somehow a bit cool. “But *I* saw *you* this lunchtime.”

Oh? And?

Then he asked: “Was that by any chance your *boyfriend*?” He sounded very **disapproving**.

I don’t like it in the slightest when people talk to me in a disapproving way, so I just said pertly: “Yes. That was Sven.”

“He isn’t called Sven,” said Sven.

I went red. Now that I found totally embarrassing. After all, I could never have guessed that he knew him.

“That’s got nothing to do with it,” I said pertly.

“Have you known him for long?”

“Of course.”

Why the great **interrogation**? I started to feel annoyed with Sven.

“And you’re still going out with him?” asked Sven, surprised.

“Why shouldn’t I? What’s all this really about?” Now I was gradually losing patience.

“Oh well, you must know what you’re doing,” said Sven.

---

for ages – ewig; disapproving – missbilligend;
interrogation – Ausfragerei

"Yes I do," I said **snottily**.

Sven shook his head. "Then I was wrong about you. I thought you were cleverer than that." With that, he went.

I was in a flaming temper. Who does that so-and-so think he is? It's got absolutely nothing to do with him whom I go out with. I went home angry.

At home Flippi informed me that she had decided not to move to England.

"I don't think it would do my slugs any good. Until they've made new friends there, and then there's the foreign language and stuff."

"Are you mad?" I cried. "We have to go to England!"

Flippi stared at me dumbfounded. "Since when have you thought that?"

"England is totally cool. Honestly!"

"**What are you on about**? You were the one who was against it!"

I shrugged my shoulders. "Well, I've had a rethink."

Strictly speaking, it was Eberhard who gave me the idea this afternoon. You see, I had told him that we might perhaps be moving to London, and he was totally **thrilled**. He was **bowled over** and said I

---

snotty – rotzig, gemein; What are you on about? – Wovon redest du?; to be thrilled – begeistert sein; to be bowled over – überrascht sein

really was a lucky cow. And he would visit me in any case. There was just one thing I had to do before I moved, and that was find someone else to take Herr Schmitt out in my place. But not that cheeky girl who had handed the dog over recently. I piped down a bit because I thought he was perhaps angry because of Flippi. But, fortunately, he wasn't.

He was totally sweet and said he was really pleased that I was always so nice about helping him with Herr Schmitt. And he also said we absolutely had to go for **a slap-up meal** sometime before I moved, or to the cinema, or both. We had to celebrate my departure properly.

Now I can hardly wait for us to move. Then he'll finally go out with me at last!

He really **envied** me going to London; he said it was completely cool of me.

I had never thought that people would find that sort of thing so great and, above all, never imagined that they would then in turn find people so great who moved to London.

So, if I've understood it correctly, I've gained cool points because we might move to London. That really is amazing.

I have to inform my mother right away that she should accept this job. And I finally have to start

---

a slap-up meal – ein Essen mit allen Schikanen;
to envy sb sth – jmdn. um etw. beneiden

reading the books she gave to Flippi and me so that we could **get a handle on** England and stuff.

Saturday 11th November

My mother was very surprised by my change of attitude, and was glad about it. "There, just look what a difference it makes if you give the country and its people a bit of thought. Then you quite quickly abandon all your **prejudices**."

"When are we moving?" I pestered. I could hardly wait to celebrate my departure with Eberhard.

"Not so fast, Jojo, first of all we'll all go to London and have a look around and see whether we'd like it there," said my mother carefully.

"Oh, I'll like it, I know I will. So far as I'm concerned, we can move right away."

My mother frowned. "Now, Jojo, don't be **over-hasty**. Not so long ago you didn't want to know anything about it and **vehemently** refused to go."

"I've just changed my mind."

"There's something behind this!"

I went red. "Nah, nothing at all."

---

to get a handle on sth – etwas kapieren;
prejudice – Vorurteil; over-hasty – vorschnell;
vehement – heftig

Saturday evening, 11th November

This afternoon was wildly romantic with Eberhard. He brought me a nougat ring again, which we ate together.

Then we bumped into Lucilla with Pooky; she didn't even dare to say hello to me. I was quite glad about it because Eberhard would otherwise have wondered why Lucilla was walking around with 'my' dog. And it's guaranteed that I'd have **come unstuck** with my Sven-Eberhard name business.

She disappeared, and twenty minutes later she was back again with Carla **in her wake**. I could see how she was going on to Carla with a triumphant note in her voice. Carla was trying to look bored, but in truth she was impressed and most definitely jealous to boot. Unfortunately Annette was nowhere to be seen; I'd have found it totally brilliant if I'd been able to show Eberhard off to her as well.

Monday 13th November

I met Annette today.

"What's the latest on Sven?" she immediately wanted to know.

---

to come unstuck – sich verraten; in her wake – im Schlepptau

I had my brain **engaged** and knew who she meant. "Everything's okay. We've been together loads."

Annette sighed. "Lucky you!"

Then I told her about London, and Annette sighed again. "You're so lucky! I wish something like that would happen to me sometime."

"What's the latest on Edgar?" I asked.

Annette beamed. "We're going to the cinema together quite often now. It's just the dog-walking that's starting to get me down a bit. For the past few days I'm supposed to be walking Mops across the field. It would be more healthy for the dog, is what he said. I think that's totally stupid actually, but when he looks at me I always give in instantly. He has such a look on his face..."

I nodded; I knew that look. Eberhard had a look like that, too. They must have been on the same course.

And then we **raved on** about Eberhard and Edgar respectively, and were in a really good mood.

Then Lucilla arrived with Pooky.

"Have you seen *him* anywhere?" she whispered to me. "I urgently need to see him again. But it has to seem like a coincidence."

I knew who she meant, and just said: "No-o-o, haven't seen him."

---

engaged – (hier:) in Gang gebracht;
to rave on about sth/sb – für jmdn./etw. schwärmen

Then I remembered my last conversation with Sven again, and I felt a bit annoyed. I don't know what that Sven **weirdo** meant. 'I thought you were cleverer.' **Tut, tut**. He's just jealous.

At last things are going really well with Eberhard.

What's more, I didn't mind that he didn't have time for me today. He had to do something with school or whatever. I wasn't at all cross. Not in the slightest.

Life is simply wonderful.

Tuesday 14th November

Life is even more wonderful than wonderful: I'm going for a **farewell** meal with Eberhard this evening. He suggested it himself! It was his idea.

I think it's really romantic. It's somehow got something truly dramatic about it: the first time is simultaneously the last time. It's like in a film. Well, of course, quite apart from the fact that it's not remotely the last time, because we're not remotely moving yet. But I just couldn't wait any longer, and that was the surest method of getting him to go out with me.

I'll just disappear off the face of the earth for a

---

weirdo – Komiker; Tut, tut – Ach was; farewell – Abschied

couple of days, then reappear and tell him we didn't like it and that we've moved back again.

Eberhard was very brave yesterday when I told him that today was the last time we'd see one another. He didn't **betray** his emotion.

"Listen," I said, putting on a serious but **composed**, brave expression. "I've got bad news for you. For both of us." Then I inserted a dramatic pause. He looked at me curiously.

I carried on speaking, acting as if I were finding it difficult. "We did know that one day the time would come…"

He raised his eyebrows **uncomprehendingly**.

"… And now this is what it has come to: we have to say goodbye," I breathed.

I simply had to say it. I had practised this sentence **for yonks** in the mirror and had put into it all the melancholy that I could **muster**.

"I'm going to London the day after tomorrow," I said almost silently so that it would sound as sad as possible.

Eberhard, however, was very composed. "Yeah, okay," he said. "But you can take Herr Schmitt out tomorrow afternoon, can't you?"

---

to betray – verraten; composed – gefasst;
uncomprehending – nicht begreifend;
for yonks – ewig lange; to muster – aufbringen

"Of course," I reassured him. No way would I **leave him in the lurch**.

I had asked Annette if she could stand in for me for a couple of days, and she immediately agreed. I thought that was totally lovely of her.

Oh well, I was truly proud of the way I'd **wangled** that one, and told Eberhard straight away.

"You don't have to worry about Herr Schmitt," I told him. "I've got a friend who'll take over for me."

He beamed. "Hey, fantastic."

"She's totally lovely. And she takes her boyfriend's dog out every day anyway. Going for a walk with two dogs makes no difference to her. So it's all settled. She's called Annette."

"What's the dog called?" Eberhard wanted to know instead.

"Mops."

"Mops?" he asked, sounding a bit **frantic**. "Um, you know, that's perhaps not such a good idea after all," he said suddenly.

"It's a brilliant idea," I informed him.

He shook his head. "Naah, just leave it, I'll sort it out myself."

Then he smiled at me really sweetly and said: "You don't have to worry your sweet little angelic head about it."

---

to leave sb in the lurch – jmdn. im Stich lassen;
to wangle – deichseln; frantic – verzweifelt

Isn't he totally sweet?! I melted. Oh, it was just really romantic.

Wednesday 15th November

What a fool. Honestly.

Yesterday I was standing in the park like a good girl, waiting for Eberhard.

He came rushing up and murmured somewhat out of breath: "So sorry, little angel, but something's **cropped up**. I can't make it tonight, I'm afraid. I've got to help my father wash the car."

"I don't believe it!" I cried, annoyed.

He was put slightly off his stroke. "You don't?"

"I just don't believe it. Something *always* crops up!" I grumbled.

He smiled sadly. "I'm very sorry. Our last evening, and then this happens."

I was quite cross and terribly disappointed. But I tried to pull myself together because I had resolved not to over-react any more if Eberhard sometimes had no time for me.

He tried to console me. "You know what? If you come back for a visit, we'll make it up straight away. Okay?"

---

to crop up – unerwartet passieren

I was offended.

He looked me in the eyes most remorsefully and smiled **timidly**.

I sighed. Oh, he really couldn't help it. And you just can't be angry with someone who can look so trusting.

"Well, there you go," he said happily and **nudged** me in the side. "I already like you better like that."

Oh, he's so-o-o sweet and so charming.

Then I remembered something and I beamed. "Hey, it's not a problem at all! I'm not moving yet!"

That totally threw him. He looked nowhere near as happy as I'd imagined.

"What? When that's the reason for all that fuss?" he cried. "You could have said so straight away."

I was irritated because he was kind of angry.

"I'm sorry," I stammered. "I must have got it mixed up." I sounded really stupid even to myself.

He sighed, irritated, and nodded his head **pensively**.

"But we could go out together tomorrow," I suggested cautiously.

He growled.

"What's the matter?" I wanted to know.

"So you presumably expect to be able to carry on doing the job with the dog, do you?"

---

timid – schüchtern; to nudge sb – jmdn. mit dem Ellenbogen anstoßen; pensive – nachdenklich

"I don't quite understand..."

"I **laboriously** go round looking for another... someone else... a **mate** to take Herr Schmitt out, and then I hear that you're not moving at all."

"I don't mind not taking Herr Schmitt out any more, honestly," I tried to help him out.

But somehow it didn't help him. I really didn't understand what his problem was.

He thought for a moment. Then he smiled sweetly again and said: "Oh well, you never know. It's all right."

I nodded. "Shall we meet tomorrow? Perhaps we could make it then for the cinema or a pizza or something."

Eberhard thought it over. "Erm, I've really got a lot on at the moment, but... tell you what: give me your phone number and I'll call you if I need you. Um, I mean if I have time. Okay?"

He wanted my phone number! Hey that really is something. I wrote it down for him and gave him the **slip** of paper.

He looked at it and nodded. And then he finally asked the question I'd been waiting so long for: "So what's your name, then?"

I was so overjoyed that I felt embarrassed and, somewhat red in the face, mumbled: "Jojo."

"Jojo? Strange name," he stated.

---

laborious – mühsam; mate – Kumpel; slip – Fetzen, Stück

Now I didn't remotely think so. And especially people called Eberhard ought to keep quiet.

"I'm called Josefine, but people call me Jojo," I said rather coolly.

He had himself back under control again and said: "Nah, you know, I mean, I like the name. Honestly. It's something a bit different." And then he smiled charmingly again. "But 'little angel' suits you even better," he added, and I melted inside.

Wonderful, sweet Eberhard! He's so-o-o-o-o lovely!

"Well, then," he said, smiling at me. "Take care. I'll be in touch." And then he stroked my hair – my platinum-blonde hair – and pushed off.

I stood there for a while longer, sighing and staring after him.

At the next corner he met a friend who gave him a **matey thump** on the shoulder – and then the pair of them headed off towards the cinema.

Towards the cinema?!

Oh well, perhaps Eberhard lives somewhere around there, or he's dropping his friend off at the cinema.

Happy, I went home.

---

a matey thump – ein kumpelhafter Schlag

Thursday 16th November

Lucilla rang me and said complete catastrophe had struck: she had messed up the last Maths test.

"And guess what my mum said," moaned Lucilla to me. "She said: 'That's it, young lady. That's an end to all that dog-walking, you're going to stay at home now and **revise**.' It's just unbelievable! And it has to happen just when I've met Sven."

"That's really tough," I backed her up.

"And the worst thing," Lucilla began again, "is that she's forced me to dye my hair back again. That has to be the limit." She started to howl.

"Don't let it get to you, Lucilla," I comforted her. "I'll help you with the **revision**, and you'll do brilliantly in the next test, and then your mum will be fine again."

"Do you think?"

"Of course." I really could be a good friend.

But to be quite honest, I was also a bit grateful to Lucilla's mother. First of all, I had had enough of playing **hide and seek** with Lucilla and Eberhard and, moreover, I also thought it was better if there weren't so many platinum-blonde girls around. Because Eberhard, after all, was keen on platinum blonde, and the fewer platinum-blonde girls there

---

to revise – (hier:) pauken; revision – Büffelei, Paukerei; hide and seek – Versteckspiel

were around, the better. I don't much like competition.

"Could you do me a favour, Jojo?" asked Lucilla suddenly.

I was slightly suspicious. "What?"

"It's about Sven."

Oh no, please not.

"Could you please tell him hi from me? I can't go out again now."

"Fine by me," I said.

"Thanks a million. You see, I don't want him to forget me."

I was annoyed that Lucilla had reminded me of him again, because I had just managed to forget about him again after quite some effort. I reckoned his last appearance was **bang out of order**.

Oh, I can hardly wait to see Eberhard again.

Thursday evening, 16th November

I went straight to the park this afternoon, but neither Eberhard nor Herr Schmitt was there. Nor, **incidentally**, was Sven. But, of course, I couldn't care less about that.

---

bang out of order – total daneben;
incidentally – nebenbei gesagt

At least Annette was there, and she was hugely glad to see me again.

"Guess what? I've met someone. She's totally lovely. You'll like her," cried Annette enthusiastically.

"Her?" I asked, astonished. Since when has it been so great meeting a girl?

Annette grinned. "Just wait – you won't believe it." She looked at the time. "She'll be here any minute. There she is!" cried Annette enthusiastically.

"What's so exciting about it?" I asked.

And then I saw: the girl had long platinum-blonde hair and a dog on a lead. I couldn't believe it: she looked like Annette and me.

"She's also taking her boyfriend's dog for a walk!" cried Annette excitedly, and waved madly to the girl. "What a coincidence! Now we're a real **clover leaf**."

"Clover leaf?"

"Well, I admit it's a strange expression; it comes from my grandmother. She always meets up with the same two friends, and the three of them call themselves the clover leaf."

I still looked blank.

"Clover leaf – three leaves," explained Annette, irritated. "Oh well, never mind. By the way, her boyfriend's called Friedhelm. Pretty stupid, don't you think? But she's called Sonja, and she really is totally lovely."

---

clover leaf – Kleeblatt

"Your grandmother's called Sonja, and she has a boyfriend?"

Annette looked at me in astonishment. "What are you talking about?" Then she **gesticulated** towards the platinum-blonde girl. Oh, right.

The 'totally lovely' Sonja came happily over to us, shook my hand, and said: "Hello, Jojo, Annette's told me about you. So where's Herr Schmitt?"

Huh, I'd like to know that as well.

Hopefully Eberhard hadn't really found a replacement for me, because it was kind of stupid going for a walk without a dog.

But I then walked along – without a dog – with the pair of them, and we had a lot of fun.

I envied Sonja her boyfriend because his dog was genuinely good looking. An Afghan. That's like a big **greyhound** with really long pale and dark hair. Looks totally cool. And seriously elegant. 'Lady,' the dog's called. Because it's a lady dog. I certainly can't keep up, what with my bodybuilder King Poodle. And you can completely forget Annette and her slobbery Mops.

Sonja had promised Friedhelm she'd drop the dog off at the **vet's**, so she couldn't stay long.

Then I wanted to wait with Annette for Edgar. As I didn't have to rush off to meet Eberhard, I had

---

to gesticulate – mit den Händen/Armen fuchteln; greyhound – Windhund; vet – Tierarzt

had a lot of spare time for a while now. I, of course, didn't have a dog. Felt almost deserted, really.

Edgar did and didn't come. At one point, Annette thought she'd seen him from a distance and waved to him, but he didn't wave back, but instead immediately disappeared again. Annette said that it most likely wasn't him and that she must have made a mistake.

It reached the point where I couldn't wait any longer, so I finally went home.

I was somehow sad about Herr Schmitt. I don't want to be the only one without a dog. I want to take Herr Schmitt out again, even if I have to search the entire town for him. And moreover: wherever Herr Schmitt is, Eberhard is there too. And I have to see him even more urgently than I have to see Herr Schmitt. I'm longing so much to see him!

Then I saw Sven of all people. I remembered that I'd promised Lucilla that I'd say hi for her, so I went up to him.

"Hello!" I said, trying to look friendly. I was somehow sorry that he wasn't so nice to me any more.

"Hello," he said coolly.

"How are you?" I asked.

"How's Sven?" he asked, giving 'Sven' a rather strange **emphasis**.

---

emphasis – Nachdruck

That annoyed me again, and I said arrogantly: "Thank you for asking. He's **magnificent**."

Sven looked at me rather sadly and said: "It's always the nicest girls who fall for the most stupid guys!" Then he shook his head and sloped off.

I thought that was totally stupid, and got genuinely angry.

I'm not saying a single word to him again.

Oh damn, now I've completely forgotten to say hi from Lucilla.

Friday 17th November

He rang! Hurrah! He loves me!

He said his friend who wanted to take Herr Schmitt out hasn't got time any more. If I wanted, I could do it again.

Let's go!

I'm totally happy.

---

magnificent – herrlich, großartig

Monday 20th November

Now everything's back to how it was before. Annette, Sonja and I have lots of fun taking the dogs out for a walk. But, unfortunately, everything really is back to how it was before: Eberhard, as ever, has no time for me. We still just meet for the dog-handover, and then that's it.

He's also becoming more and more **unreliable**, and already more than once I've been standing there with Herr Schmitt, with no Eberhard anywhere to collect him.

So I then had to go about my business dragging that idiot dog along with me.

I felt totally stupid, and so I struck a deal with Flippi: she takes the dog and gets paid for it. I offered her two euros, and I reckon she's already overpaid.

I'm already regretting entrusting the dog to Flippi, because Herr Schmitt is always totally distraught and **intimidated** after being looked after by her.

When Flippi brought Herr Schmitt back yesterday, the dog was **sopping wet**. And looked completely miserable. His beautifully blow-dried coat and his **topknot** were sticking to his body.

---

unreliable – unzuverlässig; intimidated – eingeschüchtert; sopping wet – klatschnass; topknot – Dutt

"What on earth has happened to Herr Schmitt?" I asked, horrified.

"Never heard of a '**drowned** poodle'?" giggled Flippi.

"What?"

The matter was actually perfectly logical: Flippi simply and sweetly wanted to know what a 'drowned poodle' looked like.

"Well, people do say: 'he looks like a drowned rat'," explained Flippi. "And I've never seen a drowned rat or a drowned poodle. It was a **gap in my education**."

I nodded. "So, you drowned him. But what with, for God's sake?"

"Chocolate sauce!"

"What's the matter with plain straightforward water?" I asked in desperation.

Flippi shook her head. "I can tell you never do experiments. Of course I poured water all over him first. But he shook it off. And two minutes later, he looked perfectly normal again. Then I tested various other liquids, and this series of experiments showed that chocolate sauce is the stuff that sticks best."

"We can't give him back like that!" I cried desperately.

"Why not?" asked Flippi, astonished.

---

drowned – (hier:) begossen;
a gap in one's education – eine Bildungslücke

"**Because**. **Oh blow it**, we'll have to bath Herr Schmitt."

Flippi beamed. "Great idea."

That was right up her street.

We raced back and firstly put the King Poodle under the shower and tried to get the stuff off. With our mother's apple-scented shampoo. The whole bottle went on him. And on my nerves. Because I was forced to discover that you can't just stop a dog from shaking. That's what they always do when they get wet. Must be hard-wired. Herr Schmitt shook himself with and without apple shampoo. And our bath looked like a leaking submarine.

Flippi had offered to explain everything to our mother. In return for payment, naturally. Wow, what a lot of money this dog costs me! But it's better if Flippi **takes the rap** because there's a chance of a mild punishment or even none at all.

I was totally stressed about how late it was. I jogged back without worrying any further about the flooded bath, and was already feeling quite guilty because I was so late. But Eberhard was only just arriving as well, and felt bad **likewise**.

"Sorry, little angel, for keeping you waiting so long."

Because! – Deshalb!; Oh blow it! – Ach! Verdammt!;
to take the rap – für etwas bestraft werden;
likewise – ebenfalls

"Doesn't matter," I said, rather out of breath.

He took Herr Schmitt's lead, and prepared to go. I was pretty happy he hadn't noticed anything, because Herr Schmitt stank overpoweringly of apple shampoo.

Then he suddenly stood still and said to me: "Mmm, new perfume?"

"Er, no. Yes. *Wild Apple* by ..."

He didn't wait for my answer; no doubt about it, he was in a big hurry. "Smells great. But now I really do have to go, Frau Kaltenbach is bound to be waiting for her dog."

"Frau Kaltenbach?"

He looked at me blankly. Then he quickly said: "My grandmother."

"You must be a pretty formal family. Do you have to use the polite form of the verb as well?"

"Sometimes," he cried to me over his shoulder, and ran off.

I was a bit confused, but happy that Eberhard hadn't noticed anything. And Herr Schmitt would hopefully keep his trap shut.

On the way home, I looked around for Sven. But there was no sign of him. I don't actually care where he's got to either. I just want to say hi from Lucilla.

Flippi gets on my nerves.

I asked her to take Herr Schmitt for half an hour because I had to go to the library. When I came back out, Herr Schmitt was wearing a cap.

"What's all that about? Why's the poodle wearing a cap?" I snapped at her.

"Calm down," said Flippi. "It's a poodle cap!"

"That doesn't make it any better. Take the cap off him!"

"You can do that once I'm out of sight. I was in town with the dog today, and everyone was howling with laughter behind my back. They laughed themselves silly about Herr Schmitt's curly topknot and his swept up hairstyle. So I put a cap on him."

"That looks even more stupid," I said and took the cap off him.

Flippi took the cap from my hand. "As of now, my services have gone up by the way. I demand compensation if I'm supposed to walk around with that embarrassing mutt. You've got no idea how **tiresome** it is!" Then she sloped off.

Just at the right moment, because Eberhard was already coming round the corner.

I had planned to be a bit **stand-offish** because Sonja said stand-offish was totally in. She'd carried

---

tiresome – lästig; stand-offish – kühl

out some studies and had discovered that the most stand-offish girls in her class always had a whole **pack** of boys running after them. And she said we ought to try being a bit stand-offish because we might greatly improve our chances of success. Of course I'll try it out; why not? All's fair in love and war.

So I was really cool when I saw Eberhard, and handed him the lead without a word.

"Thanks, little angel," he said, and made as if to go.

I didn't utter a word.

He remained where he was and stopped short. "Is something wrong?"

"No," I said casually, and acted as if I were about to turn and leave.

He held my shoulder to stop me. "There's something the matter?" he asked **probingly**.

"No," I answered shortly, turning my shoulder away from his hand.

He was somewhat confused. "Hey, just tell me what's the matter."

"It wouldn't interest you in any case," I said slightly pertly, starting to find the game fun.

He became nervous. "Of course it would! You know it would!"

I walked a couple of steps, and when he didn't immediately follow me, I slowed down again.

---

pack – Rudel, Schar; to probe – stochern

He was coming, thank God! He put his arm round my shoulders, and my knees went weak.

I just didn't get it! You have to be cool and **dismissive** towards boys. Then they show some interest in you. It just can't be true! What kind of stupid fools are they?

It wasn't at all difficult to act as if I were in a bad mood, because I really wasn't in the best of moods. It annoyed me that I always looked forward to seeing him so much, and then he never had time for me after all.

"So why are you in a bad mood, little angel?" he asked me **affectionately**.

I **heaved a deep sigh** of happiness.

He interpreted it differently. "It's that bad? Come on, tell me; you can tell me anything."

My heart beat like mad, he still had his arm around me, and we walked beside each other like a couple. I was in seventh heaven.

Now a dramatic story just had to occur to me very quickly so that I could **prolong** the whole thing a bit. I hadn't remotely counted on it being so easy and working out straight off. That's why I hadn't got a story ready.

Ha, Annette and Sonja should just see me now. They'd be amazed! I'd actually have liked to have

---

dismissive – abweisend; affectionate – liebevoll, anhänglich; to heave a deep sigh – tief stöhnen; to prolong – verlängern

seen myself. The two of us, that is. We were undoubtedly a handsome couple. I tried surreptitiously to steal a glance in a shop window so that I could have a look at us. The fact that in so doing I had to turn my head away from him fitted in perfectly.

"Look at me, little angel," said Eberhard gently.

I'd have given my life to look at him, but I couldn't do so yet because my **camouflage** would be **blown**. One look into his eyes, and I'd be done for. I looked desperately in the opposite direction and remained silent.

"Is it because of Herr Schmitt?"

I shrugged my shoulders and gradually started to panic. What on earth had I started? I really didn't know what to do next. How could I get myself out of this again?

"Don't you want to take him out any more?"

Okay, I had made a decision. I would stop walking, turn to him, and look deep into his eyes. Then he would kiss me.

"Don't you want to go for a walk with Herr Schmitt any more?" he asked gently.

"Yes, of course I do," I answered equally softly. Now the kiss just had to come. I waited.

Eberhard removed his arm from around my shoulders, took a step back, and breathed a sigh of relief. "Thank God. I'd started to worry!"

---

to blow one's camouflage – seine Tarnung opfern

He beamed.

I was utterly flabbergasted. What was going on?

He thumped me heartily on the shoulder and said: “Brilliant! See you tomorrow, then!” And with that, he disappeared.

The stupid **ass** went away. Just like that. Instead of kissing me, he thumped me on the shoulder and pushed off.

Was that normal?

As if **in a daze** I walked home, reliving what had happened scene by scene. Where had I made a mistake? What went wrong? And it all started so well!

Perhaps he was just too shy! I had to give him a second chance to kiss me.

Oh, but kiss or no kiss, he put his arm round me! For quite a long time. And it felt so-o-o brilliant. That’s something. That’s actually a whole lot!

If he didn’t like me a lot, he’d never do anything like that in his whole life. What do I mean, ‘like me’? He’s totally mad about me.

Do you wanna bet?

I absolutely have to tell my mother to turn down the London job. I can’t move now, when I’m just **on the brink** of my first kiss with Eberhard.

---

ass – Esel; in a daze – betäubt; benommen;
to be on the brink – haarscharf davor stehen

Wednesday 22nd November

Is my family stupid or what?

My mother is reluctant to promise that we won't move to England. She said they'd given her six weeks to think it over, and she was going to use these six weeks, and she wasn't going to be pressured by me into making a decision. Yeah right, she'd rather ruin her elder daughter's life. Oh great.

And Flippi really is a complete prat. She wants to split me and Eberhard up. She's always making **snide** remarks.

"You're **as thick as a plank**, Jojo! Can't you see what's going on here?"

"Leave me alone, Dumbo. It's got nothing to do with you."

"Oh, nothing to do with me, eh? After all, I'm related to you, and when word gets round that you've got the intelligence of a goldfish, it'll all reflect upon me!"

"I haven't the **faintest** idea what you want!"

"Oh, just open your eyes, just engage your last bit of brain. Love surely can't make you so-o-o stupid!"

"Now say it in words of one syllable!"

Flippi looked at me pityingly. "Do I really have to say it more clearly?"

---

snide – abfällig; as thick as a plank – strohdumm;
faint – schwach, gering

"Please do!"

She took my arm and pulled me onto my bed. "Well," she began, as if she were talking to a patient.

"Don't talk to me as if I were sick," I snapped.

She rolled her eyes. "You *are* sick, Jojo. Lovesick!"

I jumped up angrily.

"But – good news. It's not **incurable**. Sit down again and listen."

"No," I said defiantly and remained standing. I did want to hear what Flippi had to say, but I at least wanted to remain standing.

Flippi took a deep breath. "You've fallen for a **confidence trickster**!" she said, and held her breath in order to await the effect of her words.

There was no effect. I had no idea what she was talking about.

Flippi boldly continued. "Your Sven – and I doubt that's his real name …"

I went red.

"… isn't in the slightest bit interested in you. He's just pretending to fancy you so you'll go on taking the mutt out. And, by the way, I doubt that it's really his dog."

"It's his grandmother's dog," I interrupted in order to salvage whatever could be salvaged.

"If he actually has a grandmother."

"Everyone's got a grandmother!"

---

incurable – unheilbar; confidence trickster – Hochstapler

"Jojo, Jojo!" My sister shook her head. "What on earth will become of you?

"Don't be so **smarmy**. Was that all? Was that what you were making such a palaver about?"

Now Flippi turned quite direct. "The guy got you to dye your hair and take a completely ridiculous dog out every day. And in my opinion, you're not the only one. He's got a whole pack of girls who take out a whole pack of dogs. And it's guaranteed that he lets the dogs' owners pay him for it. He's making a load of **dosh** out of it, sister dear! And it's possible that all his hens have dyed their hair blonde for him."

I wasn't prepared for this, and I felt slightly sick. Now I had to sit down after all.

Could Flippi be right? Could sweet, charming Eberhard really do something so **rotten**?

"You think about it," said Flippi and **slammed** the door behind her.

I collapsed and sobbed. I always howl when I don't know what to do next. It's quite good, because at least I've got something to do.

After careful consideration I came to the conclusion that Flippi was completely off her head, and that not one single word she'd said was true.

Then I already felt better. I cooled my tear-

---

smarmy – pathetisch; dosh (slang) – Knete;
rotten – faul, mies; to slam – knallen

stained eyes with a wet flannel and set off defiantly. Set off to see Eberhard. No way would my sister part us! True love is **indestructible**. Or does love in fact make you blind after all? I know it makes you blonde: I proved that myself after all.

Oh, rubbish! These are just all the fantasies of a **precocious** creature who reads too many detective stories.

I could barely speak to Eberhard; I was afraid that otherwise he'd be able to tell that I'd been hearing such terrible things about him. And he was so sweet. He's generally been a lot nicer to me recently. He's mad about me, it's obvious.

Isn't it?

Then I walked in the park with Annette and Sonja.

I was desperate to think about something different.

"Why did you two actually dye your hair platinum blonde?" I suddenly asked, without wanting to ask it.

Sonja said at once: "Because it's totally in."

There you go. It's 'in'. Precisely. That's what I said.

Annette giggled. "Edgar got me to do it. He said platinum blonde would definitely suit me."

Shock.

Sonja nodded. "Friedhelm's keen on platinum blonde, too."

---

indestructible – unzerstörbar; precocious – altklug, frühreif

That was that. My freshly raised hope **withered** again.

I confessed miserably: "I also only dyed my hair because of Sven."

"So what? Why are you saying it so miserably? It doesn't matter!" said Sonja cheerfully.

"But don't you see what it means?" I cried, **infuriated**.

They both looked at me, astonished.

"Well?" I inquired. "Just think about it for a moment!"

"Love is blonde," giggled Sonja.

"Yes, and blind!" I cried.

Annette frowned with annoyance. "Say, what's wrong with you, Jojo? Are you looking for an argument?"

I shook my head and sank down onto a park bench. "I don't exactly know how to explain it, but I'd very much like to meet Edgar and Friedhelm sometime. Just to be sure."

The pair of them looked at one another. "She's completely **lost her marbles**," said Sonja to Annette.

Annette shrugged her shoulders. "I don't know what her problem is."

I looked at them both helplessly. "I don't exactly know what my problem is either. But somehow I'd

---

to wither – verdorren; infuriated – außer sich vor Wut;
to lose one's marbles – verrückt werden

like to make sure that we haven't all got the same boyfriend."

Sonja and Annette half killed themselves laughing on the spot.

"You watch too much television. Hey, this is real life!" said Sonja cheerfully.

"Okay," I cried, eager to do battle. "Then prove it to me. Fetch Friedhelm here!"

Sonja was indignant. "I'm not having you tell me what to do."

"Ha, you're afraid!" I cried triumphantly.

Annette tried to **mediate**. "Jojo, stop fantasising, just calm down."

Sonja took Lady and said: "Take your stupid dog out on your own. Anyway, it's embarrassing to be seen with a mutt like that, all **crimped** and **permed**." Then she turned to Annette. "Come on, Annette, we're going."

"Oh, so it's not embarrassing for you to be seen with a slobbering bulldog called Mops?" I cried angrily.

Only when Annette gave me an offended look was it clear that this hadn't been a good move. Now I'd managed to hurt Annette as well.

Annette turned and walked away with Sonja. Shaking her head.

---

to mediate – den Vermittler spielen; crimped – gekräuselt; permed – dauergewellt

I shook my head too. How had that happened again? I had lost two friends in the space of a few minutes.

How on earth does that happen? Exactly: it was Flippi's fault. All just because of Flippi! Stupid kid. **She's had it**.

After I'd returned Herr Schmitt and was back at home, I made Flippi explain herself.

I angrily told her about the disaster, but she just rolled her eyes. "They're even more stupid than you are! Know what? We'll prove it to them. Okay?"

"Exactly! We'll prove it to them," I cried enthusiastically. "But how?"

Flippi smiled, **confident** of success. "Just leave it to me."

"Thank you," I said.

When Flippi had gone, I thought it all through again. Had I just said 'thank you' to my own sister? To my little, chaotic, completely **insane** sister?

I'd genuinely imagined that the conversation would take a different course. So what happened *this* time? Why is my life rushing past me, and why are things happening which I have no influence over? Why don't I ever have things under control?

She's had it! – Ich werd's ihr zeigen!;
confident – selbstsicher, zuversichtlich;
insane – verrückt

And why am I now stuck in the same boat as Flippi, **joining forces** with her of all people? And against who exactly? Surely not against sweet, charming Eberhard, who always calls me angel. I love him, after all!

Why is everything in my life always so complicated?

And whose fault is it, may I ask?

I'm not sure, but I reckon it's my mother's.

What's more, I'm still pretty cross about Sven. First of all he's totally nice to me, then he behaves completely stupidly. And now it's as if the ground has swallowed him up. Well, not quite. He's just no longer in the places where we used to bump into one another.

But Lucilla is up to date. She lies in wait for him in town, at the **filling station**. But he's mostly in the library, she says.

She's found out that he's also at the Humboldt, in the year below Eberhard. That makes me really angry. Hasn't she got anything better to do than chase after a guy? Lucilla really annoys me. Her mother shouldn't have lifted her house arrest. It'd be better if Lucilla did more for school.

Obviously he's good-looking; obviously he's really nice and funny. But so are lots of people.

---

to join forces – sich zusammenschließen;
filling station – Tankstelle

But there's one thing she still hasn't managed yet: he hasn't been for an ice-cream with her again.

Sven is actually even nicer than Eberhard. And I think that's really mean.

Life is so unfair!

Thursday 23rd November

Flippi returned from her first **reconnaissance** trip as an amateur detective today and said, somewhat **disgruntled**: "That so-and-so is smart. He **gave me the slip** twice."

"Well, you can't blame him, what with the way you look!"

Because Flippi had disguised herself: she was wearing our mother's trench coat and – as if that weren't already bad enough – she had also stuck on a **moustache**. She's nuts, this sister.

"But we've got our first proof: when he took Herr Schmitt back, I managed to follow him discreetly."

Discreetly: if you believe that, you'd believe anything.

---

reconnaissance – Erkundung; disgruntled – verstimmt;
to give sb the slip – jmdm. entkommen;
moustache – Schnurrbart

"And do you know where he took him? To one of those **posh** houses, to a completely **tarted-up** woman who gave him money for it. Ha!"

"Even so, it could still be his grandmother!"

"Pah, if that's his grandmother, I'm your brother."

"Flippi, that doesn't prove anything at all. I'll never be able to convince Annette and Sonja with that. That's the end of the clover leaf and stuff," I said **despondently**.

"Clover leaf? Have you been hanging around with botanists, or what?"

"Oh, forget it. That's another story. So where was he while I was **roaming around** with Herr Schmitt?" I asked Flippi.

"Don't know. I told you, he shook me off. But he wasn't at the children's home. I was there. No Sven anywhere to be seen."

"Eberhard." I thought I should tell Flippi the truth. "He's called Eberhard."

"Ugh, Eberhard. All this palaver for someone called Eberhard. Jojo, Jojo." Flippi shook her head. "I bet you anything he's not called Eberhard either."

I looked at Flippi, baffled.

"There's no way he's called Eberhard. You're such a silly goose. So why did you always call him Sven?"

---

posh – vornehm; tarted-up – aufgedonnert;
despondent – ohne Hoffnung, niedergeschlagen;
to roam around – herumstreunen

I didn't say anything.

Flippi looked at me, then she started to laugh. "You made up a name for him because you thought Eberhard was too embarrassing. That really has to be a great love. Wow, are you stupid, Jojo!"

"Now, you control yourself, or you'll be out of a job!" At the end of the day, I was paying for Flippi's **snooping**.

"Private detectives aren't short of work, you know. If I were in your position, I'd be nice to me."

I **bit back** a suitable answer and returned to the matter in hand. "So how do we proceed from here?" I asked Flippi.

"I'll shadow Annette tomorrow," Flippi informed me grandiosely. "I just need a different disguise. The coat is too long; I tripped on it three times, and **came a** complete **cropper**. By the way, here's the bill for the plaster." With that, she gave me a sales receipt. Which also included the price of a bar of chocolate.

I held the receipt up. "What's that all about?"

"**Expenses**," said Flippi. She shrugged her shoulders, and disappeared from my bedroom.

I hate that little **rascal**.

Besides that, I'm noticing that I like Eberhard less and less. And that's the most irritating thing of all.

---

to snoop – schnüffeln; to bite back sth – sich etw. verkneifen; to come a cropper – hinfliegen;
expenses – Spesen, Unkosten; rascal – Schlingel

Friday 24th November

I saw Sven. He was in the library. I had to go there anyway. That is, I wasn't there because of Sven.

He acted as if he didn't want to see me, but I went up to him all the same, because of course I had to say hi to him from Lucilla. She may not be under house arrest any more, but I had after all promised her that I'd say hi.

I was a bit embarrassed, and just said: "Hey, I don't want to keep you long, but Lucilla asked me to say hi. You see, she has…"

"I'm not interested in Lucilla," he interrupted me.

"No?" I was surprised. I was very glad about it, but wasn't so sure exactly why.

"You just don't get anything, do you?"

I stood there rather stupidly and looked at him. He turned back to his books and acted as if he had to concentrate hard on them now.

So I went away again.

If he liked me, he wouldn't just let me go, would he?!

Stupid guy.

But it's good that he's not mad about Lucilla. Otherwise he'd have faced a huge disappointment. Because Lucilla's got a new flame. Some guy or another who works in a music shop and who, of course, is supposed to be really swee-e-e-t.

I had asked her indignantly what was going on

with Sven, then, and she did actually give me a completely surprised look before saying: "Sven?"

"Yes, Sven, the guy you think is so great. The one who caught my dog again," I helped her out.

Lucilla laughed. "Oh, him. Yeah. You know, I don't think he's so great any more. You'd have to see this guy from the music shop, Jojo! Really swee-e-e-t!"

"I thought that Sven was pretty great," I defended him.

"Then you can have him," said Lucilla in an **offhand** manner.

"Oh honestly," I acted outraged.

"Oh yeah," Lucilla then cried. "Of course – you've already got a Sven. I'm all confused." She giggled. "This guy is honestly **well-cool**. You've absolutely got to come to the shop with me."

"Yeah, yeah," I said, and went.

"Of course – you've already got a Sven," Lucilla had said. You must be joking. I haven't. I haven't even got an Eberhard if I carry on like this.

---

offhand – kurz angebunden; well-cool – ober-cool

I've thought it all through quite precisely once again. It's complete nonsense. Flippi and her fantasies!

Eberhard is totally lovely to me. And he looks so sweet. And he is cool. And it's precisely because he's so helpful that he has so little time.

Now I've lost Annette and Sonja because of Flippi, and if I don't watch out, it'll all be over with Eberhard too before I know it. I'll tell my sister she's to stop her stupid detective business on the spot. Her theory is completely wrong.

And I have to have a sensible conversation with my mother again in peace and quiet about London. I don't want to move there. I want to stay here.

That's what I did straight away, and my mother said: "I've started to doubt whether it's the right decision for us too. We all feel quite happy here, and I like my work at the theatre. I think I'll **turn it down**."

"I'm glad you've come to your senses," I said approvingly to my mother.

Her eyes became angry. "Jojo, you know, you sometimes have a way of saying things that really annoys me!"

---

to turn sth down – etw. (z. B. ein Angebot) ablehnen, abschlagen

"So what have I said now?" I snapped at her.

She sighed. "I'll be glad when you've got through puberty."

"Puberty? Ha, that's nothing compared to having to live with you two. You're always getting at me, you've always got something to moan about. And Flippi's totally nuts, and makes my life hell!"

"Child, you're **exaggerating beyond measure**. I really do try to **summon up** understanding for you, but sometimes..."

"You don't try at all," I interrupted. "You only understand Flippi."

And with that, I rushed out of her room and into my own.

And I'm going to stay here until I'm eighteen and can move out.

Life is utterly stupid.

Monday 27th November

Stupid isn't remotely the word for it.

Flippi came home to report her most recent discoveries to me.

I yelled through the door to her that she should

---

to exaggerate – übertreiben; beyond measure – maßlos;
to summon up – zusammenraffen/aufbringen

disappear and leave me alone. "I don't want to hear anything about your sick fantasies! If you'd not got involved, everything would be dreamy."

"Nightmarish," retorted Flippi. "You're as blind as you are blonde! I actually wanted to break the news to you gently …"

I laughed **scornfully**. If you believe that, you'd believe anything!

"… but you don't deserve any better. I was right. Everything is exactly as I thought it was. The so-and-so has a whole pack of girls and a pack of dogs. While you **plonkers** are dragging the mutts all over the place, he's hanging out with his mates laughing himself to death. His theory is: If you can get a girl to dye her hair blonde, then she's also stupid enough to take a completely strange dog out for a walk. And because it works so well, he has three girls at once who earn money for him. So, that's it."

I **wrenched** the door open. "I don't believe a word of it!"

Flippi just looked at me.

"Have you got proof?" I shouted at her.

Flippi kept looking at me, and for the first time I noticed something sympathetic in her eyes. "I'm kind of sorry, Jojo," she said, and put her hand on my arm.

As she was going, she turned round again. "Oh,

---

scornful – höhnisch; plonker (leicht vulgär) – Torfnase, Blödmann/-frau; to wrench – aufreißen

by the way: he's called Jens. He just invented the strange names **to make fun of** you."

I collapsed, sobbing. Even without any proof, it was suddenly obvious to me that Flippi was one hundred percent right.

I dragged myself over to my bed and moaned loudly. That was it. My life was over. Everything is so awful. However could Eberhard be so mean! Eberhard?

No, Jens!

Jens, alias Eberhard, alias Edgar, alias Friedhelm.

Oh God, we really are – how did Flippi put it again? – as blind as we are blonde!

Oh wonderful. So that's what happens when you fall in love. I'll never fall in love again. That was absolutely the last time.

I hate being in love! However could I be so stupid?

Once I had just managed to calm myself down a bit, it struck me that the whole business was dreadfully embarrassing as well. It was well-embarrassing. Deadly embarrassing. 'I-have-to-leave-the-country' embarrassing.

Then something struck me.

I jumped up and ran to my mother. "We're moving to London! Preferably today!"

My mother was just making our supper. That is to say, she was spreading Nutella on bread. When I an-

---

to make fun of sb – jmdn. veralbern

nounced our move, she was so taken aback that a piece of bread fell out of her hand.

She was most probably about to react in an irritated way, but then she must have seen my **tear-stained** face, and took me in her arms. "Jojo, darling, what's the matter?" she said tenderly.

That really annoyed me. I immediately freed myself. "Nothing's wrong. I just want to go to London. At once."

I could see how my mother was making an effort to think what the correct pedagogical reaction would be, so I said, in order to **ward it off**: "Just don't give me all that puberty and stuff again. I've given it careful consideration."

My mother had already opened her mouth to speak. She quickly shut it again. "Fine, that's all clear. Don't get worked up," she said, trying to calm me down. But whenever my mother tries to calm me down, it has the opposite effect: I become angry.

"You don't understand me anyway," I grumbled, and I saw how my mother could only just manage to **suppress** rolling her eyes.

Quite gently and carefully, she attempted an approach. "Go on, just try it for once. Give me a chance."

I snorted. Well fine, she could have her chance. "Okay. What would you do if someone was totally

---

tear-stained – verheult; to ward sth off – etw. abwehren; to suppress – unterdrücken

mean and dishonourable to you, and then made fun of you?"

My mother frowned and thought. "I think I'd try to talk to them. I'd make them explain themselves, and would tell them that their behaviour was very hurtful and offensive to me."

Ha, there we were again. That woman has no idea! I rolled my eyes.

My mother became bolder. "So what has happened? Is it about Sven? What's the problem?"

Again, that annoyed me beyond measure. She is always snooping around in my private life. "Nothing has happened, and it's got nothing remotely to do with Sven. I simply wanted to tell you that I would like to move to London. But of course you always immediately have to make some problem or another out of it." And with that, I left her alone with her bread and Nutella.

That wasn't particularly successful; I didn't feel **an iota** better.

I went to see Flippi in her room.

"I just wanted to tell you that we're moving to London," I said shortly.

Flippi shook her head. "That's stupid. You can't just get lost and let the so-and-so get away **scot-free**."

"I don't want to get lost, I just wanted to inform

---

an iota – kein bisschen;
scot-free – ungeschoren

you that we're moving. Anyway, I'll certainly still talk to him sensibly and explain to him that his behaviour is completely antisocial."

Flippi gave a scornful laugh. "You must have a screw loose. Talk to him! Who does that sort of thing?"

I was somewhat perplexed, especially when I heard myself say: "Oh, what would you do then?" I surely can't be asking my little sister for advice!

Flippi's eyes lit up. "Ha, I'd take **revenge**. Furious, dreadful revenge. I'd make his life hell. That's what I'd do."

Revenge?

Revenge! Yes. That was it.

The very thought of revenge instantly made me feel better.

"I would never **stoop** to such a level," I said **loftily**, and rushed out of Flippi's room.

Revenge! Yes, brilliant!

I will get my revenge.

It's just a matter of how.

For that, I need to come up with something really good. Afterwards I can of course still always move to London.

---

revenge – Rache; to stoop – sich herablassen, sich bücken; lofty – erhaben, hochmütig

Tuesday 28th November

Can you believe it? I didn't come up with anything.

I was forced to discover that I had no idea of how you get your revenge. Great, I've had no practice at that either. Neither at being in love, nor in finishing with someone, nor in **forging** plans for revenge. Thirteen years old and utterly unable to **cope with** life. Well, hasn't my mother done a great job of bringing me up? Congratulations!

Now that doesn't get me any further either. For however I twist and turn things, I can't **sweet-talk** Eber-… er, Jens, any longer.

I can think of nothing other than revenge, and I can't think of any way to get my revenge.

A kingdom for a revenge plan!

"And what are you going to do?" Flippi burst into my room this morning.

I knew at once what she was talking about. "Huh, I'm not going to the park any more. Then he'll soon see how far it's got him."

Flippi roared with laughter. "Great revenge, you **novice**."

I **pouted**.

---

to forge – schmieden; to cope with sth – mit etw. fertig werden; to sweet-talk – schönreden; novice – Anfänger(in); to pout – schmollen

"Of course you're going. Right now!"

"Hey, listen, after all…"

Flippi didn't even let me finish. "You go and act as if you knew nothing at all. Be friendly and charming. How are you going to get your revenge otherwise?"

"Great revenge, being friendly and charming."

"That's not the revenge, you plonker!"

"Oh. So what, **pray**, does the revenge look like?" I asked, irritated.

Flippi pulled a worried face. "I've also been going over it in my head the whole time. Nothing brilliant has occurred to me yet. It has to be something huge. Something that destroys him **with one fell swoop**!"

My mother really should keep an eye on what sorts of films Flippi watches on TV. She sounded positively scary.

"But I'll think of something. You can **bank on** it," she said, and left my room.

Then she stuck her head round the door once more. "Let the other **blondies** know. This has to be a team effort."

That wouldn't be so easy. I hadn't seen either of them since our argument that time.

---

pray – (hier:) bitteschön;
with one fell swoop – mit einem Schlag;
to bank on sth – sich auf etw. verlassen; blondie – Blondine

Now, though, there was nothing for it. I had to talk to Annette and Sonja and get across to them how stupid we three are.

But that's not all. I'll also have to go to see Sven. And apologise to him as well. What do I mean, apologise? But I should at least talk to him. He did after all try to warn me about Jens. Didn't he? Oh, I don't know any more. Whatever, I have to see him urgently.

Tuesday evening, 28th November

I had decided to look for Sven **first off**. So I walked through the town and through the park, and when I saw him, I got a shock of delight and almost didn't dare speak to him.

But then I pulled myself together and gave myself a good talking to. It had to be easy now!

I ran up to him. "Have you got a moment? I'd very much like to talk to you."

He nodded.

"It's about … I mean…" I **fumbled for words**. He grinned, and all of a sudden I found it quite easy to

---

first off – gleich am Anfang;
to fumble for words – nach Worten suchen

say that I'd behaved pretty stupidly, and that Jens was an absolutely **crummy** guy and stuff.

Sven laughed, put his hand on my shoulder, and said: "I'm glad you worked that out for yourself. True, I could have told you all that as well, but there's no way you'd ever have believed a word I'd said."

"Of course I'd have believed you," I said at once.

He gave me a penetrating look.

"I wouldn't have done," I then admitted **sheepishly**.

"You'd definitely have thought I just wanted to **run him down** because I'm **head-over-heels** in love with you," said Sven.

"You're what?" I cried. And a feeling of total happiness flowed through me.

He was in love with me! It's incredible!

Sven betrayed no expression. He acted as if it were the most natural thing in the world to tell a girl almost as an afterthought that you're head-over-heels in love with her.

"Is it true?" I asked once again to be on the safe side. I mean, before I start rejoicing like mad here and now, I'd rather be certain.

---

crummy – ätzend, schäbig;
sheepish – schüchtern, verlegen;
to run sb down – jmdn. heruntermachen;
head-over-heels – (hier:) von Kopf bis Fuß

Sven made a totally innocent face. "What?"

"Well, that..." I broke off. That was just totally embarrassing. I couldn't possibly repeat that he was head-over-heels in love with me. That's what he had said. Or had I misheard?

"Er... what you just said," I stuttered, embarrassed.

"Everything I say is true. I may not remember what I said, but I'm pretty sure that every word of it is true." Sven's expression was totally harmless, and I became quite unsure.

Only when he grinned at me did I know that I hadn't misheard. He was head-over-heels in love with me.

I was pretty confused. But confused in a good way. Good-mood-confused.

"What on earth are we going to do now?" I asked.

"What do you mean?"

"Well, with Eber-... er, Jens?"

Sven raised his eyebrows. "You want advice from me about what you should do about Jens?"

"Well, why not?"

He shook his head. "No-o, I don't think so. You've got yourself into this; it's nothing to do with me. You have to sort it out on your own."

I did find that a bit hard. I mean, first he says he's in love with me, and then he won't even help me with Jens.

I pouted.

He laughed, bent down to me, and gave me a kiss

on the cheek. “Keep me in the picture,” he said, and **strolled off**.

I held my hand to my cheek in exactly the place where he had kissed me, and thought I was going to faint. That was just unbelievable.

It’s possible that I’m a lucky cow after all, and that everything will turn out fine.

Handing over the dog this lunchtime was really difficult for me, because what I’d really like to have done was scream at this Jens-Eberhard – and in a way that would have made his hair stand on end, the stupid idiot!

But I didn’t. I took Herr Schmitt and my face betrayed no expression towards Jens.

But the nitwit didn’t even notice a thing. In any case he’s far too busy finding himself fantastic to **take in** anything else. Unless someone sets a firework off or bites him on the nose. Then he might perhaps notice something. What a complete fool!

Then I saw Annette and Sonja and went up to them. And they weren’t at all cross with me, and we walked through the park as always.

Bit by bit, I came out with the whole Jens story. But they still wouldn’t believe it.

I had to tell them about Flippi’s shadowing activ-

---

to stroll off – davonschlendern;
to take in sth – etw. mitkriegen

ities in **minute** detail. Which was a bit awkward for me. After all, it concerned my little sister. And that she of all people should have more **nous** than three almost-adults, *is* embarrassing. But of course we are blonde. Platinum blonde.

"How can she be so certain, then?"

"Because he said so himself!"

"Friedhelm?" said Sonja.

"Jens," I corrected her.

"Edgar told your little sister this?" Annette inquired incredulously.

"Jens! He's called Jens. And of course he didn't tell her. He told his friends."

"And your sister was standing next to them by some strange coincidence?"

"Of course it wasn't a coincidence!" I cried. And then I told them Flippi's story in minute detail.

Flippi had followed Jens into a pizzeria. This was evidently along the lines of a favourite pub for Jens and his friends.

His friends were already waiting for him.

"What's new on the blondes front?" one immediately called to Jens, and Flippi at once came and stood by their table.

The boys looked questioningly at Flippi and

---

minute – haarklein, winzig;
nous – Grips

asked if she couldn't go and stand around somewhere else because they wanted to talk.

"I'd like to do that as well, but I just happen to work here," said Flippi **brazenly**.

"Child labour is banned," said some Mr **Hypershrewd**.

And Flippi answered: "I'm helping my uncle out; that *is* allowed. So, give me your order please."

"We've already ordered."

"That's not my problem," said Flippi easily. "So …?"

Of course, the guys stopped talking and **rattled off** their order again, which was pretty stupid.

Flippi nodded and went to the next table so that Jens could deliver his report.

"Have your blondes still not **twigged** yet?" one asked.

"Not in the slightest – they're blonde after all," cried Jens, and they all **cracked up**.

At the neighbouring table, Flippi wiped the table a bit with her handkerchief. In doing so, she disturbed a young couple who actually wanted to be alone. But Flippi wouldn't be Flippi if she were bothered by something like that.

The man said they had already ordered.

---

brazen – dreist, unverfroren; hyper-shrewd — superschlau; to rattle off – herunterleiern; to twig – kapieren, schnallen; to crack up – grölen

Flippi answered that may well be so, but some people changed their minds, so she wanted to ask once more just to be sure that the order hadn't changed, and to double check what they had actually ordered.

"It's the best job I've ever had," she heard Jens laughing at the next table. "No work, and pots of money!"

At the table which Flippi was still working away at, the girl **tamely reeled off** what they had ordered, and Flippi said she would pass the order on to the kitchen if they were really sure that their order would stay the same.

The girl had started to waver a bit and said: "Perhaps I'd be better off with a salad."

"Salad? Do you know that you're **depriving** lots of innocent snails of the whole basis of their existence by eating salad?" said Flippi indignantly.

Now the girl was distinctly unsure. "Well, all right, maybe I won't take the salad."

"Very good," said Flippi.

Jens started to be aware of Flippi, and stopped talking. In order not to **jeopardise** her disguise, Flippi moved to the next table and cleared up there.

Unfortunately, the people hadn't yet finish-

---

tame – zahm, brav; to reel off – herunterbeten;
to deprive sb of sth – jmdn. um etw. berauben;
to jeopardise – gefährden

ed eating, and immediately complained **vociferously**.

Flippi kept her cool, merely saying: “Sorry, I can’t make allowances for that, we need the plates.”

Two tables further on, someone called to her to say he’d like a Coca-Cola.

Flippi called back: “Good idea, so would I!”

In the meantime, Jens told the whole story again, and the boys enjoyed themselves enormously.

Then the owner of the pizzeria – Flippi’s ‘uncle’, that is – appeared and asked if there was a problem.

Flippi shoved a plate into his hand and said: “I **resign**!”

“That’s just not true!” said Annette tonelessly and sank down onto a park bench.

“Yes, she really did say she was resigning,” I assured her.

Annette waved me aside. “I don’t mean that.”

Oh, right.

“What now?” she asked.

I beamed, because here was my chance: “Now it’s revenge time!”

Sonja shook her head. “Wow, is that embarrassing! If it ever gets out, then we’re done for permanently. God, how embarrassing!”

“It certainly is!” I nodded.

---

vociferous – lautstark; to resign – kündigen

Sonja sat down on the bench next to Annette and said nothing at all for a while. Then she looked at me.

"Okay, Jojo, **count me in!** Our slogan is revenge! What's your plan?"

I beamed, then I became slightly embarrassed. My plan? I didn't have one. Flippi had one. That is, perhaps she had one, hopefully she had one. If something had occurred to her in the meantime. Could I say that? I mean, that we have to wait for an eight-year-old to come up with a brilliant revenge campaign? Embarrassing, embarrassing. Nah, I'd rather not.

"Well, we'll meet here tomorrow. Don't give anything away; collect the dogs from Jens and act as if nothing were wrong. I've got to go now. Sven, er... Jens, needs Herr Schmitt back a bit earlier today."

I had to leave quickly because I didn't want to admit that I didn't have a revenge plan. But in the first instance, it was a matter of whether the pair of them were going to be involved or not.

"Tell me," said Sonja suspiciously. "Why did he actually invent a normal name in your case? Sven sounds pretty good – Edgar and Friedhelm really are the pits."

I went red. Bright red.

Quite sheepishly I admitted: "He told me he was

Count me in! – Auf mich kannst du zählen!

called Eberhard. I just called him Sven because I thought Eberhard was so dreadfully embarrassing."

Sonja nodded and laughed in recognition. "You're pretty damned clever, Jojo. I'd never have thought of that idea."

I shrugged my shoulders. Now, I wasn't exactly clever. I just have a low embarrassment **threshold**. I find *everything* embarrassing. Even names.

Then I suddenly remembered the non-existent revenge plan again. "Well, I really do have to go!" I cried. "See you tomorrow." And then I **made to** leave.

"Hey!" Annette shouted after me. "So what's happening tomorrow? Do we have to wear anything special, do we have to prepare anything or whatever?"

"Nah, it's not necessary."

At least I hope not.

Now everything depends on Flippi. My fate depends on my little sister. Oh great. She'd better have the idea of the century now, or I'm absolutely **done for**.

I had arranged to meet Sven after the dog-handover, and was there a quarter of an hour early because I couldn't wait to see him. But I didn't stand around for long because he was early as well.

---

threshold – Schwelle;
to make to do sth – sich anschicken, machen, dass;
to be done for – dem Schicksal ausgeliefert sein

"Our watches both seem to be fast," he cried cheerfully, and greeted me with a kiss on the cheek.

I enjoyed it and didn't say anything, but beamed at him.

"Ah," he said when he saw me beaming. "A good-mood day."

"It certainly is," I nodded. "You absolutely have to come to the park tomorrow. We've come up with something really bad for Jens."

"What, then?"

I shrugged my shoulders. "Don't know."

Sven stopped short and then started to laugh. "So who *does* know?" he asked.

"My little sister. She's the world's best **hatcher** of revenge plans."

Sven laughed again and put his arm around me. "Come on, let's go and have a pizza."

"I'd love to," I beamed.

I was ecstatic. Sven really was totally sweet.

We walked in the direction of the pizzeria, Sven giving me sidelong looks the whole time.

I became really nervous and didn't know what to say or do.

"You're quite some chaotic **chick**," he said then.

I looked at him, annoyed.

"But really sweet," he pacified me.

I was more than pacified; I was utterly delighted.

---

hatcher – Aushecker; chick – Küken, Mieze

"And I think you're really fantastic – cool and funny," I said. It was quite easy to say it. Because I also meant it.

Sven stopped walking, looked me in the eyes, and grinned. "Prove it!"

"How?" I asked, irritated.

"Well, by…"

"Hey, Jojo, I'm glad to see you! I've had an idea. Quick, get a move on, we've got to buy something. I need twenty euros," someone behind me suddenly bawled, and then I felt Flippi tugging at my arm.

Sven and I sprang apart, shocked.

He cast a look at Flippi, laughed, and then said to me: "Your sister. Am I right?"

I nodded. And felt madly annoyed with Flippi.

"But I've got something else planned!" I hissed at her.

"Postpone it. Revenge is more important!" stated Flippi.

Sven laughed again. "I agree with her."

That won him an approving look from Flippi.

I wasn't very happy about this course of events, and felt completely fed up. What on earth was Sven doing, taking Flippi's side?

"Quick, come on now, the shops are about to shut!" Flippi pestered me.

Sven gave me an utterly lovely look. "We'll postpone the pizza, okay?"

"Good boy," said Flippi to Sven and **patted** him on the shoulder.

"**Paws** off, Flippi!" I cried.

"You two definitely spend too much time with dogs," stated Sven.

He was one hundred percent right about that one.

I did in fact allow myself to be **persuaded** by Flippi that at that moment nothing was as important as tackling her plan for revenge, and I set off with her.

When Flippi and I got home in the evening, my mother was standing in the kitchen repeatedly wiping the same bit of the stove, shaking her head and mumbling to herself. She took no notice of us.

Flippi and I were very irritated. The thing is, wiping the stove clean is very unusual and in any case unnecessary. How's it supposed to get dirty? It's never used!

We tried to catch some of her mumblings. As she kept saying the same thing, we were able to hear it quite clearly the seventh time: "I'm as thick as a plank," moaned our mother.

Now Flippi and I really were **flummoxed**. Flippi comforted our mother. "You can't help it. You've probably got it from Jojo. It runs in the family."

---

to pat – leicht klopfen; paw – Pfote; to persuade sb – jmdn. überzeugen; to be flummoxed – verblüfft sein

I gave Flippi an angry look.

Our mother sighed. "I'm really sorry about London, for causing you such a lot of stress."

"It's okay," we generously forgave her. "It's all sorted now."

"No, not really," she said sheepishly. "I got into a muddle about it. When the director asked me if I wanted to work for him, I thought he meant in London because he works at a London theatre. But when I called to reject the offer today, it turned out that he's going to New York. And he wants to take me there with him."

"Oh, New York? Makes no difference, we'd decided against moving anyway," I said.

"Well, we'd decided against London. But what do you **reckon to** New York?" asked our mother hopefully. She looked at our horrified expressions and quickly said: "Well, do at least have a think about it. I've got a couple of books about the city and the people and their customs."

Flippi and I looked at each other in horror. Now we were starting right back at the beginning again!

"Well, I think we should at least give New York a chance," said our mother, and stopped wiping.

"But I don't want to move!" I moaned.

I can't leave the country when things are just starting to develop with Sven!

---

to reckon to sth – (hier:) von etw. halten

Wednesday 29th November

"Just you be on time," Flippi warned me this afternoon as I set off to take Herr Schmitt out.

"Are you really sure that Mum won't be at home?"

"Quite sure," Flippi reassured me. "I've sorted out an appointment for her with my Textiles Design teacher."

"Does your teacher know about the appointment?"

"Of course not, what do you think? The last thing I need is for Mummy to get together with my teacher."

"But Mum will notice sooner or later that your Textiles Design teacher isn't there."

Flippi brushed me aside. "No problem. First of all she'll do the right thing and wait, and by the time she realises that no one is coming, it'll be so late that she'll only just manage to get to the theatre on time. Today's the **dress rehearsal**. We've got the place to ourselves for the whole afternoon."

I shook my head. Flippi took everything so calmly and easily.

But she's bound to come unstuck sooner or later.

When I met Annette and Sonja with the dogs, they immediately bombarded me with a ton of questions.

---

dress rehearsal – Kostümprobe

"My little sister Flippi has sorted something out. It costs twenty euros. We'll have to split it."

"What's she got planned?"

"I can't say." I had promised Flippi I wouldn't tell them what she had planned.

"Ha! Your little sister. Oh fantastic. *Flippi*! What sort of name is that?" Sonja made fun of it.

I looked at Annette **beseechingly**. But Annette also looked suspicious. "Why are you leaving something so important to your little sister?"

I looked the pair of them straight in the face. "Because, of all the people in the world, only she can make the most absurd things happen. If you want Flippi to do something, all you have to tell her is that it's impossible, and bingo! She makes it possible. She's not afraid of anything, and has ideas that nobody has ever had before. She doesn't stick to the rules, not even the laws of nature! Believe me. If there's a perfect revenge plan, then Flippi has it."

After my **fiery** declaration I was left **downright** speechless about myself. I had said really nice things about my sister. What on earth was wrong with me? Puberty really didn't suit me.

Sonja and Annette weren't quite so convinced. But as they didn't have any ideas of their own, they came back to my house with me.

---

beseeching – anflehend; fiery – feurig;
downright – ausgesprochen

Three dogs, three platinum-blonde blondes – I prayed that my mother wouldn't appear.

When we got to our flat, I couldn't believe my eyes. Flippi had rearranged the decor. It looked like a hairdressing salon.

Flippi was wearing a white overall and greeted us like a professional. "Ah, the three-fifteen appointment, **bang on time**. Very good. If you'd like to follow me, please," she piped, and dragged Herr Schmitt into the bathroom.

When she emerged again half an hour later, we all let out a scream. Initially one of shock, then one of delight.

Herr Schmitt, the black King Poodle, was platinum blonde. Exactly like us.

Flippi is simply a genius!

She then dyed Mops and Lady platinum blonde too. Annette and Sonja were so thrilled that they didn't just give Flippi the money for the hair dye, but gave her five euros on top.

"Your **tip**," they giggled.

I was immensely proud of my little sister. Jens would have a few difficulties this evening explaining to his customers what he'd done to their dogs. He would lose his jobs and would get into enormous trouble.

Flippi wanted to hand the dogs over to him. All

---

bang on time – absolut pünktlich; tip – (hier:) Trinkgeld

three at once. And we were to stand in the background smiling and waving at him most charmingly.

Flippi had planned it all right down to the last detail. She really is a gem!

Now quick, let's go!

Eberhard-Edgar-Friedhelm is waiting.

We three blondes had also sworn a **sacred oath** in advance of the encounter, namely that we would never fall in love again as long as we lived.

Wednesday evening, 29th November

It was an absolute hit!

Flippi was already waiting in the park with the dogs and was to **appear on cue**.

Sven was leaning casually on a lamp post, watching the whole thing from a distance. I **winked** at him as I walked past him, and he winked back.

Jens was already there, waiting impatiently. Annette, Sonja and I walked up to him arm in arm.

He turned pale when he saw us together.

"Hello, Jens," we cried cheerfully.

---

sacred oath – heiliger Schwur; to appear on cue – rechtzeitig (auf der Bühne) antreten; to wink – zwinkern

Jens didn't utter a sound.

"Nice to see you!" we cried.

"Where are the dogs?" he asked coldly.

We three looked at one another. "The dogs? What dogs?"

Jens turned even paler.

"Oh, *those!*" we then said. And grinned. "We've got a surprise for you. You're bound to be delighted."

Jens lost even more colour.

We **chirped** on. "You're so keen on platinum blonde, and so we thought..."

Now Flippi could make her entrance. She came with all three dogs. Platinum-blonde dogs!

Jens's eyes widened, and he gasped for air. "What have you done to the dogs?" He went bright red and was completely **beside himself**.

It was fabulous! Jens was raging around like Rumpelstiltskin, completely unable to calm himself down.

We almost died of laughter.

"You stupid cows," he cried, trying to wrench the dogs' leads from Flippi's hand.

Flippi, however, had already let go, and the dogs ran off into the park. Like good dogs, each one in a different direction. You couldn't possibly have rehearsed it any better.

---

to chirp – säuseln; to be beside oneself – außer sich sein

"Whoops," said Flippi to Jens with an innocent expression. "I'm so sorry. I don't think you should have said that stuff about cows. I was so shocked that the leads slipped out of my hand. How silly of me."

Jens stormed off after the dogs, utterly stressed out because he didn't know which one to **pursue** first.

We just couldn't stop laughing.

Sven, likewise, almost killed himself laughing. Then he came over to me, took me in his arms, and said to us: "That was really fantastic. A great operation. We have to celebrate! I'm inviting you all for a pizza."

"And I'm inviting *you* to Rome," he said quietly and rather tenderly to me.

Then he put his arms round me more tightly and kissed me.

"Ugh!" cried Flippi, and turned away.

Annette and Sonja looked on wide-eyed. "But Jojo!" they cried. "What about our oath?"

I hadn't a clue what they were talking about.

My knees went weak.

Oh wow, oh wow. He is magnificent. Honestly.

He's perfect. Ideal. He's a knockout.

I'm totally crazy about him.

---

to pursue – verfolgen

Von Hortense Ullrich bei Thienemann
bereits erschienen:

Hexen küsst man nicht (1)
Liebeskummer lohnt sich (2)
Doppelt geküsst hält besser (3)
Liebe macht blond (4)
Wer zuletzt küsst ... (5)
Und wer liebt mich? (6)
Ein Kuss kommt selten allein (7)
Unverhofft liebt oft (8)
Ehrlich küsst am längsten (9)
Never Kiss a Witch

Ullrich, Hortense:
Love is Blonde
Aus dem Deutschen von Helena Ragg-Kirkby
ISBN 3 522 17763 0

Reihengestaltung: Birgit Schössow
Einbandillustration: Birgit Schössow
Texttypografie: Marlis Killermann
Schrift: New Baskerville
Satz: KCS GmbH, Buchholz/Hamburg
Reproduktion: Medienfabrik, Möglingen
Druck und Bindung: Friedrich Pustet, Regensburg

5 4 3 2 1*   05 06 07 08

Thienemann im Internet: www.thienemann.de